THE POETRY OF
GERARD MANLEY HOPKINS

THE POETRY OF
GERARD MANLEY HOPKINS

A Survey and Commentary

BY

ELSIE ELIZABETH PHARE

(Mrs Austin Duncan-Jones)

CAMBRIDGE

AT THE UNIVERSITY PRESS

1933

CAMBRIDGE
UNIVERSITY PRESS

University Printing House, Cambridge CB2 8BS, United Kingdom

Cambridge University Press is part of the University of Cambridge.

It furthers the University's mission by disseminating knowledge in the pursuit of education, learning and research at the highest international levels of excellence.

www.cambridge.org
Information on this title: www.cambridge.org/9781316611975

© Cambridge University Press 1933

First published 1933
First paperback edition 2016

A catalogue record for this publication is available from the British Library

ISBN 978-1-316-61197-5 Paperback

To

MARGARET MASTERMAN

PREFACE

THIS account of Hopkins's poetry does not pretend to be complete; in particular, it contains no analysis of his prosody, a subject with which I am not competent to deal and which, in any case, seems likely to be amply dealt with elsewhere.

I owe thanks to Newnham College, Cambridge, as it was while I was holding a Marion Kennedy Research Studentship there that the essay was begun: to Dr I. A. Richards for the help and encouragement which he has liberally given me: to Miss A. D. M. Hoare and to Mr and Mrs Richard Braithwaite for reading the manuscript and proofs: and to Mr E. H. Blakeney for supplying me with references to Milton.

I must also thank the Delegates of the Oxford University Press who have been very generous in allowing me to quote freely from Hopkins's poetry and from Fr. Lahey's *Life*, as well as to quote a poem by R. W. Dixon and a poem by Robert Bridges. The Librairie Gallimard has kindly allowed me to quote from the poems of M. Paul Valéry, and Payot et Cie to quote a passage from M. Étienne Gilson's *La Philosophie du Moyen Âge*.

I am also indebted to Messrs Faber and Faber for permission to quote the poems of T. S. Eliot and to Messrs Chatto and Windus for permission to quote from Mr Empson's *Seven Types of Ambiguity*, and from Mr Huxley's *Music at Night*.

ELSIE ELIZABETH DUNCAN-JONES

University College
Southampton
August 3rd, 1933

THE POETRY OF
GERARD MANLEY HOPKINS

I

The French, an orderly nation, like to begin the study of a poet by considering the place which he should take in the ranks of the poets as a whole. It is possible in Paris to find a bookseller's window placarded with the discovery that the place of Lautréamont, for instance, is between Rimbaud and Baudelaire. There is something to be said for this habit. Nothing, certainly, is more difficult than to make a study of a poet's work in complete isolation: to consider it purely as and for itself. The approach is made very much easier if, to begin with at any rate, we make an effort to see it beside the works which it most resembles. Sometimes these will be the works of contemporaries: sometimes of poets who are distant from him in point of time but connected with him by some sort of temperamental affinity.

With Hopkins this is extraordinarily difficult. No bookseller's window, so far as I know, has ever been placarded with the discovery that the place of Hopkins is between So-and-So and Such-and-Such; and we may doubt whether it is likely to be; at any rate for some time. There was never a more difficult case for the literary historian who likes to see literature as a chart of tendencies and groupings in which every poet finds his place. There is no group of names with which his is inevitably associated; it is with hesitation that we describe him as a Victorian— almost one of the loosest classifications imaginable— since, although Hopkins lived from 1844 to 1889, most of his poetry was published for the first time in 1918, and it is generally taken to belong in spirit and by adoption to the twentieth century. On the other hand, there is certainly no warrant for describing this Jesuit poet as a Georgian or as a post-Georgian. Using a classification based on one of the most obvious and superficial characteristics of his poetry, we might choose to associate him with the other poets of his time who were experimenters in prosody: Patmore, notably, and Bridges. Or we might couple him with Browning as a poet who founded his rhythms on common speech and disregarded conventional syntax. It is true that from time to time in Hopkins's poetry we come across lines or short passages which strikingly resemble Browning, such, for instance, as

"But how shall I...make me room there
Reach me a...Fancy, come faster—
Strike you the sight of it? Look at it loom there,
Thing that she...there then! the Master,
Ipse, the only one, Christ, King, Head:
He was to cure the extremity where he had cast her."

But there is no Victorian poet whose innovations strike the eye as odd, bizarre, far-fetched, in the degree that those of Hopkins do; and none in effect, it may be added, whose actual accomplishment in modifying our poetic vocabulary is comparable to

his. It would scarcely occur to a reader unacquainted
with Hopkins to identify such lines as

"For earth | her being has unbound, her dapple is at
    an end, as-
  tray or aswarm, all throughther, in throngs; | self ín
      self steepèd and páshed—qúite
Disremembering, dísmémbering, | áll now"

as the work of even the most experimental of
Victorians.

The fact that Hopkins spent his life from the early
twenties onwards under the discipline of Loyola may
perhaps have contributed something to his singu-
larity; as a Jesuit he was necessarily to some extent
a man apart. The fact that his poetry bears so few
marks of his age suggests that his name should be
associated with those of the other poets who in
every century have occupied themselves with themes
drawn from Christian dogma and experience; that
not very large group, in English, which includes the
Jesuit Southwell, Quarles, Herbert, Donne, Crashaw,
Vaughan, Traherne, Smart, Patmore, Christina
Rossetti, Alice Meynell, T. S. Eliot, and some others.
But the whole content of Hopkins's verse is not
devotional. As one critic has already said, we do not
feel that Hopkins's poetry springs directly out of his
religious vocation. Temperamentally he seems to
have been, like Donne,

"Apollo's first, at last the true God's priest"

(although actually, no doubt, the poet in him was
kept in subordination to the Jesuit). To call Hopkins a
devotional poet would be to suggest that the religious

(3)

element in his poetry accounts for all that is most remarkable in it: which is not by any means the case.

How, then, is this bizarre, difficult, Modernist-Victorian poet to be approached? With whom shall we compare him? A number of affinities have been suggested. Dr Bridges several times associates him with Milton, and this is a comparison which deserves consideration, particularly as Hopkins himself seems to give it countenance. In a letter of 1879 he writes: "My poetry errs on the side of oddness. I hope in time to have a more balanced and Miltonic style". I do not take Hopkins to mean more than that he hoped in time to master his own modification of the English language as completely as Milton had mastered his. There is little likeness between the modifications in question: in many respects they compose an antithesis: Hopkins's version, for instance, exaggerates the English or Anglo-Saxon element in the language, as Milton's exaggerated the Latin.

"Delightfully the bright wind boisterous ∣ ropes,
  wrestles, beats earth bare
  Of yestertempest's creases; in pool and rut peel
    parches
  Squandering ooze to squeezed ∣ dough, crust, dust;
    stanches, starches,
  Squadroned masks and man-marks ∣ treadmill toil
    there
  Footfretted in it"

is one of many passages in Hopkins which with their appearance of rough vigour, their insistent heavy alliteration, their delicate rhythm which resolves what at first strikes the ear as monotony into innumerable delicate separable tones which bring back to the reader's mind any impressions of Anglo-Saxon poetry that he may have. There is not on the face of it much likeness between Hopkins's modification of English and that which produces such passages as the following:

"Hear all ye Angels, Progenie of Light,
  Thrones, Dominations, Princedoms, Virtues,
    Powers,
  Hear my Decree which unrevok't shall stand.
  This day I have begot whom I declare
  My onely Son, and on this holy Hill
  Him have anointed, whom ye now behold
  At my right hand: your Head I him appoint:
  And by my self have sworn to him shall bow
  All knees in Heav'n and shall confess him Lord:
  Under his great Vice-regent Reign abide
  United as one individual Soule
  For ever happy; him who disobeyes
  Mee disobeyes, breaks union and that day
  Cast out from God and blessed vision, falls
  Into utter darkness, deep ingulft, to place
  Ordaind without redemption, without end."

Even so, a surprising number of resemblances can be made out. Milton's fondness for using a series of words which are almost puns:

               "...Begirt the Almighty throne
Beseeching or besieging..."
"famish him of breath, if not of bread..."
"At one slight bound high overleaped all bound"
"And feats of war defeats", etc.,

is considerable enough to provide the searcher with a number of lines which might be made out to foreshadow Hopkins. But the likeness so established would not be a great one. In fact this fondness for marking the progress of a thought by the progress of sound may be found in most poets who have used the language as virtuosos: semi-puns of this kind are to most English poets what grace-notes or warbles are to pipes: things desirable in themselves.

It is interesting to compare Hopkins and Milton as modifiers of the language. No one will dispute that Milton deserves the title. "Through all his greater works", says Johnson, "there prevails a uniform peculiarity of diction, a mode and cast of expression which bears little resemblance to that of any former writer: and which is so far removed from common use, that an unlearned reader, when he first opens his book, finds himself surprised by a new language." Addison says that our language "sunk under him". There is a general feeling that Milton, in indulging his desire to use English words with a foreign idiom, did a disservice to the poets who succeeded him. Johnson blames and acquits him in the same sentence. "Of Milton it may be said what Jonson says of Spenser, that 'he wrote no language' but has formed what Butler calls 'a Babylonish dialect' in itself harsh and barbarous, but made by exalted genius and extensive learning the vehicle of so much instruction and so much pleasure, that, like other lovers, we find grace in its deformity." T. S. Eliot, however, looking at Milton as one of a long chain of English poets, describes him as having in his blank verse erected a Chinese Wall; that is to say, having done something which makes further progress on the same lines impossible.

Now Hopkins's modification of English cannot be explained by his desire to use English words with a foreign idiom, or even with an Anglo-Saxon idiom. Even if he read Anglo-Saxon it is unlikely that he read enough of it to give him an ear which could tolerate no other cadences. There is no analogy here between Hopkins's relation to Anglo-Saxon and Milton's relation to Latin. Hopkins's version of English, unlike Milton's, was created almost entirely by personal idiosyncracy, and the ultimate source is usually Hopkins himself. In prosody, too, in spite of his appeal to Greek and Latin lyric verse, to Piers Plowman, and the choruses of *Samson Agonistes*, it seems that he was really very much a law to himself. His prosodical rules are elastic enough to make it possible to justify any collocation of syllables: it looks as though the ultimate appeal was always to his own ear.

Finally, it seems likely that Hopkins's treatment of the language is likely to have results very different from those which followed on Milton's modification of English. Hopkins, as far as can be judged, has done posterity a signal service: so far from setting up a Chinese Wall, he has broken down several barriers which no longer served any purpose: and the publication of his poetry in 1918 has left English poetry in a condition which seems to have many new possibilities.

Hopkins and Milton, then, have little in common: but there are, I think, two poets with whom Hopkins has enough in common to make it possible to institute a comparison. These are Crashaw and Wordsworth: names rarely found in conjunction. It might be permissible, I think, to describe Hopkins as a poet who combines the ingenuity of imagery, something too of the rather forced, excessive, sweetness of the most florid of English poets with the wide, pure, and, in a sense, unsophisticated sensibility of the poet of Nature. It is not only by his ingenious, exaggeratedly logical intellect that Hopkins resembles Crashaw; there is also a likeness of tone, more easily caught than defined, a likeness which is audible, I think, in such a pair of stanzas as the following:

Hopkins:

"Had she a quince in hand? Yet gaze;
Rather, it is the sizing moon.
Lo, linkèd heavens with milky ways!
That was her larkspur row.—So soon
Sphered so fast, sweet soul?—We see
Nor fruit, nor flowers, nor Dorothy."

Crashaw:

"Hark, she is called, the parting hour is come.
Take thy farewell, poor world, heaven must go
    home.
A piece of heavenly earth, fairer and brighter
Than the chaste stars, whose choice lamps come to
    light her

While through the crystal orbs, clearer than
    they,
She climbs, and makes a far more milky way.
She's called; hark, how the dear immortal dove
Sighs to his silver mate, 'Rise up, my love,
Rise up, my fair, my spotless one:
The winter's past, the rain is gone,
The spring is gone, the flowers appear,
No sweets, but thou, are wanting here.'"

The early poem from which I have quoted—it was
written while Hopkins was still at Balliol—shews
that Hopkins's poetry is at times "conceited" in the
sense in which that term is applied to the poetry
of the Metaphysical School; and it is, of course,
chiefly by this aspect of his work that he resembles
Crashaw, who is said to be the most baroque of all
seventeenth-century poets. Dr Praz describes the
baroque mentality as one which saw the universe
under the likeness of conceits; which discovered
mysterious witticisms in every aspect of heaven and
earth, and sublime symbolic meanings in every
living creature. One need only take such a poem as
The Blessed Virgin compared to the Air we Breathe in
order to see that this mentality was very much that
of Hopkins. By another side of his work, however—
though this is a comparison that cannot be taken
very far—Hopkins has some affinity with Wordsworth; and the two sides of his nature are sometimes
seen to be in conflict. Hopkins's sensibility revolts
from the thin, methodical conception of the universe
which is forced on him by his intellect. As a symptom of this revulsion it may be noticed that "wild"

in Hopkins's poetry is nearly always a term of praise:

"Wild air, world-mothering air"

is the rapturous opening of the poem which I have quoted as shewing his likeness to Crashaw. This reminds one that Alice Meynell, herself the least spontaneous of poets, said nevertheless that the poetry which she liked best was characterised by a quality only to be described as wildness. The explanation may perhaps be that as to the urban civilised mind of the eighteenth-century gardener a wilderness seemed a delightful thing, so to the tidy, cut-and-dried mental world of the Jesuit, a thing that is wild is valuable merely on account of its naturalness, its unaccountableness. By his intellect everything is seen as tidy, orderly, part of a pattern; the world as viewed in the light of Catholic dogma is a riddle solved. In his poem on *Dun Scotus's Oxford* Hopkins describes the theologian as *an unraveller of reality*: the activity of the philosopher is directed towards reducing the complexity of reality into a single comprehensible design. The same is true of the baroque religious poet; the Crashaw who works out a detailed comparison between the new-born Christ and the rising sun, the Hopkins who likens the Blessed Virgin to the air we breathe, are doing very much the same thing. But there is also the Hopkins who in such poems as *Inversnaid* and *Pied Beauty* rejoices in wild Nature as providing an antidote to the dullness and flatness which one imagines would characterise a world which had been made entirely comprehensible.

> "What would the world be, once bereft
>   Of wet and of wildness? Let them be left,
>   O let them be left, wildness and wet;
>   Long live the weeds and the wilderness yet"

he exclaims in *Inversnaid*.

Pied Beauty is the poem which expresses most clearly Hopkins's joy in the irregular and uncertain, the exceptional, all the things which cannot be rationalised, which are outside the scope of logic. Alphonsus, King of Aragon, is said to have found fault with his Maker for the untidy way in which the stars are scattered over the heavens; Hopkins, on the contrary, is particularly thankful for those features of Nature which do not accommodate themselves to our ideas of order. Possibly the virtue which Hopkins ascribes to the incomprehensibility of Nature is something like that which Wordsworth finds in her impersonality: both may be described as "healing".

From the sight of that which is individual, odd, not conforming to a pattern, Hopkins derives especial pleasure. He likes everything that hovers between two categories, such as the couple-colour of the skies, things which are now swift, now slow; things that are fickle, that vary over time; things that are freckled, that is, that vary over space. These things seem to him to be in a special way characteristic of God, because only he understands the principle on which they work.

It follows naturally from this that Hopkins should also find relief in the fact that there are some parts of life in which our activities cannot be classified as right or wrong, that there are things on which it is useless for the intellect to exercise itself in moral judgment. This is true, for instance, of the work of art; a notion which Hopkins expresses in the curious fragment called *On a piece of Music*.

> "Therefore this masterhood,
> This piece of perfect song,
> This fault-not-found-with good,
> Is neither right nor wrong.
>
> No more than red and blue,
> No more than Re and Mi,
> Or sweet the golden glue
> That's built for by the bee."

A third instance of this is the fact that Hopkins evidently takes pleasure in the thought that every man is unique and that all his actions and words have an indelible and unmistakable character; his own trade-mark is, as it were, stamped on everything that issues from him.

"As kingfishers catch fire, dragonflies dráw fláme;
As tumbled over rim in roundy wells
Stones ring; like each tucked string tells, each hung
        bell's
Bow swung finds tongue to fling out broad its name;
Each mortal thing does one thing and the same;
Deals out that being indoors each one dwells;
Selves—goes itself; *myself* it speaks and spells,
Crying, *Whát I do is me; for that I came.*"

The dapple of which he is so fond is the irregular pattern made by varying units; in the terrible *Spelt from Sibyl's Leaves* he sees as in a nightmare the day—*dies irae dies illa*—when right and wrong, black and white, are categories from which nothing is excluded. The darkness, swallowing up the dapple of twilight, drowning all colours and all shapes becomes to him a foreshadowing of the day of wrath as it was foretold to Aeneas by the Cumaean Sibyl; the beak-leaved boughs standing out against the sky take him in imagination into the dreadful future, take him, as the golden bough took Aeneas, down to hell.

II

If Hopkins is to be discussed in terms of other poets the first to be dealt with is undoubtedly Crashaw: and at the beginning it must be admitted that the points at which Hopkins resembles Crashaw are apt to be his weakest. Possibly it is because in so many respects he parts company with Crashaw that his work as a whole is so much more satisfying and significant than Crashaw appears to be even to his warmest admirers. In the first place Hopkins sometimes accepts, sometimes rejects, a way of looking at the world which is always congenial to Crashaw. Crashaw, it seems, never has any doubts of the usefulness of his favourite mental activity, which is to discover more and more proofs of the fact that divine Providence has seen to it that there shall be a certain

consistency in the whole of human experience; so
that the tiniest details become capable of being
related to the backbone of the scheme, the main
clue of the puzzle, which is Christian dogma.
How significant it is that there is a constellation
called the Milky Way! how admirably that fits in
with the apotheosis of the Infant Martyrs.

"Go smiling souls, your newbuilt cages break.
 In Heav'n you'll learn to sing ere here to speake
 Nor let the milky fonts that bathe your thirst
          Be your delay:
 The place that calls you hence is at the worst
          Milk all the way."

How neatly the meaning of our idiomatic phrase
"to cast in the teeth of" combines with the fact that
one of the most overwhelming proofs of his divinity
which Christ gave to a hostile and unbelieving world
was the multiplying of the five loaves and two
fishes!

"Now, Lord, or never, they'll believe on Thee
 Thou to their teeth hast proved thy Deity."

Crashaw's poetry is certainly injured by the pre-
dominance of the ratiocinative faculty, or whatever faculty it is that produces tissues of comparisons
as ingenious as they are insignificant. As a consequence of the fact that much of his poetry cannot be
read without producing in the reader a sense of
strain, since the seventeenth century his readers
have tended to ignore the acrobatics of Crashaw's
ingenuity, taking images which were meant to

(14)

exercise the fancy to be merely random couplings which, however rich they may be in suggestion and association, involve none of the brainwork that Crashaw intended them to provoke. Francis Thompson evidently read Crashaw in this way: "a Shelley manqué" is what he calls Crashaw, and Shelley's imagery exercises the intellect scarcely at all.

Hopkins's early poetry, like much of Crashaw's, is given an air of triviality by an excess of shallow imagery. To take a particular example from the later version of his poem on St. Dorothea:

> "Ah dip in blood the palmtree pen
> And wordy warrants are flawed through.
> More will wear this wand and then
> The warped world we shall undo."

The martyr's palm in the space of four lines becomes a pen, a wand, and something resembling a button-hook, something that will undo a twisted world: or perhaps in the third line it becomes not a button-hook but a magician's wand, magical in its effect. *Margaret Clitheroe*, an undated fragment, shews the same fondness for a succession of shallow metaphors:

> "Fawning fawning crocodiles
> Days and days came round about
> With tears to put her candle out."

Her enemies are only like crocodiles in that they feign to weep when they are about to devour. The ludicrous last line needs no comment. (It should be remembered that the poem is given as an unfinished fragment.) The nightmarish picture of crocodiles crawling round a lighted room I suppose might be appropriate to the martyr's state of mind, but Hopkins has not made it appropriate to poetry: he has been content only to startle, as Crashaw constantly is. There are other poems of his—*The Bugler's First Communion* is an example—which are spoilt by the presence of one image after another which does nothing more than startle, which will not melt away into the consistency of the poem as a whole, but stays undissolved, a lump in what should be a smooth paste.

When Hamlet remarks that a cloud is backed like a whale it is because he intends to give the impression that he has lost his wits. Otherwise the remark would have been too trivial to be worth while, and that however like a whale the cloud may have been. The far-fetched comparisons of Donne and Herbert can be justified on the grounds that they are symptoms of an attempt on the poet's part to unify the whole of his experience. I doubt whether the same can be said of Crashaw: his fondness for far-fetched and shallow comparisons is symptomatic rather of an attempt to impose a specious unity from without. Crashaw's poetry is the poetry of a man who is by no means at one with himself. He does not write as though the whole of his power were working in unison. It is true that he is not content to give pleasure only by ingenuity: and that the images with which his intellect makes such vigorous play are often overtly or covertly

sexual: but as a rule he does not achieve the equipoise between intellect and sense at which presumably he aimed. Too often his poetry leaves the
reader with the feeling that the senses have been fed
too richly and the intellect worked too hard. Possibly
the poet hoped to provide energy to the latter by
overfeeding the former: a vain hope. A journalist
once suggested that people whose minds were fixed
on spiritual things should normally be expected to
eat more than other people, simply because they
have more need of processes which keep them
attached to Mother Earth. Crashaw's devotional
poetry is based on a rather similar and perhaps not
very much less crude system of compensations: with
the result that his poetry gives the impression that
it has proceeded from a mind which, whatever
merits it may have possessed, was gravely inharmonious. I do not mean that his poetry is not
musical: it is. What it lacks is organic harmony. In
the terminology of the critics of the Romantic
Revival, it is the work of Fancy, not of Imagination.

It seems likely that the whole of Hopkins's
poetic progress may be summed up in the passage
from Fancy to Imagination. The lack of balance,
the shallowness, the febrility of the *Wreck of the
Deutschland* give place to the poised, deep, calm of
The Windhover, *Spelt from Sibyl's Leaves* and the
"terrible" sonnets, in which the poet writes and the
reader, if he is scrupulous, responds with the whole
man. Herbert Read suggests in his *Form in Modern*

Poetry that fancy may be identified with phantasy proceeding from the unconscious as a balance or compensation for instincts repressed in the interests of character. This is a suggestion which would fit in with Hopkins's circumstances; and, adopting it, one would say that while he was undergoing the arduous process of becoming a Jesuit, while his personality was having a character imposed upon it, he was not at one with himself and his poetry in consequence bore marks of a mind which, if not sick, was in some way flawed: not whole and not mature. But when use and custom and perhaps grace had combined to make character and personality coincide, the useless, unfruitful conflict which spoiled his earlier poems disappeared. The poet who could manage and control such an experience as that described in *The Windhover* and *Carrion Comfort*, who could make great poetry out of spiritual desolation and mental depression combined was one who had a very deep well of health to draw upon. Those of his poems which can be said to be spoilt, in Dr Bridges's phrase, by a naked encounter between sensuousness and asceticism are in the minority. Hopkins achieved the equilibrium for which Crashaw strove vainly. He seems to have managed a satisfactory union not only of sense and intellect but of sense and spirit.

III

Hopkins's poetry can sometimes be read in such a way that it affords the kind of pleasure which we expect to derive from Augustan poetry, and yet in his best poems he appeals to the hidden associative tangle of thought and feeling, as much as any poet of the Romantic school. It may be that in this is his peculiar strength; for evidently it is a great virtue in a poet that he should combine the characteristics of what Dryden called "wit-writing" with the depth and richness and pronounced "tactile" and visual qualities of romantic poetry.

It may be worth while to compare Hopkins's poetry with that of some of the poets of the Romantic Revival. There are evidently some points in which his poetry is not unlike that of Keats. In his schoolboy exercise, *A Vision of the Mermaids*, the debt to Keats, the Keats of *Endymion*, is obvious:

"But most in a half-circle watch'd the sun;
And a sweet sadness dwelt on everyone;
I knew not why,—but know that sadness dwells
On Mermaids—whether that they ring the knells
Of seamen whelm'd in chasms of the mid-main,
As poets sing; or that it is a pain
To know the dusk depths of the ponderous sea
The miles profound of solid green, and be
With loath'd cold fishes, far from man—or what;—
I know the sadness but the cause know not."

Again, Robert Graves in his *Poetic Unreason*[1] says that the "tactile" quality of Keats and his appeal

[1] Published by Cecil Palmer.

also to the senses of taste and smell is what most recommends the poet to him. I doubt whether even Keats appeals as strongly to these senses as Hopkins does. It is easy to illustrate: one might quote the whole of *Elected Silence* as being full of phrases which appeal to touch and taste:

> "Palate, the hutch of tasty lust,
>   Desire not to be rinsed with wine:
>   The can must be so sweet, the crust
>   So fresh that comes in fasts divine!"

> "O feel-of-primrose hands, O feet
>   That want the yield of plushy sward—"

The sloe-metaphor in the *Wreck of the Deutschland* indicates that Hopkins possessed a sensitiveness of palate and a relish of palatal sensations not less than that of Keats, of whom it is recorded that he put pepper on his tongue to bring out the coolness of the claret. Mr Graves quotes some lines from Keats's *Song About Myself* where, giving the experiences of a naughty boy, who ran away to Scotland the people for to see, he rings the changes as follows:

> "He found
>   That the ground
>   Was as hard
>   That a yard
>   Was as long
>   That a song
>   Was as merry
>   That a cherry
>   Was as red
>   That lead
>   Was as weighty", etc.,

(20)

and comments that "while this is, as it were, a succession of singles notes throughout Keats's work, one can find stanzas and single phrases which are chords struck on two or three different sense-appeals at once". This is even more evidently true of Hopkins. He is rarely content to appeal to a single sense; his own senses seem to be interconnected in an unusual degree. In a descriptive journal which he kept as a young man he writes that "the sober grey darkness and pale light was happily broken through by the orange of the pealing of Milton bells"; a passage which is interesting as forestalling Rimbaud, with his sonnet on the colours of the vowel sounds and the contemporary American poets who favour such lines as "great bells ringing with rose". In *Spring* he speaks of the cuckoo's song which

"Through the echoing timber does so rinse and wring
    The ear, it strikes like lightnings to hear him sing",

describing the sound first in terms of touch and taste —rinsing, and then with, "strikes like lightnings," in terms of sight and touch at once. There is no great virtue in "synaesthesia", as the Americans call it, merely as synaesthesia. Like any other poetic device, it can be used badly or used well. It has been used deliberately merely for its novelty by some of our contemporaries, as I think it never was by Hopkins, who is rarely conscious of his innovations, which as a consequence have an air of inevitability from their first introduction. The use of synaesthesia, however, was scarcely an innovation; as Mr Max Eastman observes in his book *The Literary Mind*[1] it dates from the *Rig-Veda*, "the fire cries out with light", though perhaps it has not often been used as unsparingly and as deliberately as it is by Miss Sitwell in her *Aubade*:

> "Jane, Jane,
> Tall as a crane
> The morning light creaks down again—
> Each dull blunt wooden stalactite
> Of rain creaks, hardened by the light
> Sounding like an overture
> From some lonely world unknown
> The light would shew, if it could harden
> Eternities of kitchen garden,
> Cockscomb flowers that none will pluck
> And wooden flowers that 'gin to cluck."

Miss Sitwell is so conscious of the novelty of the device that she provides an explanation. "The author said 'creaks' because in a very early dawn, after rain, the light has a curious uncertain quality as though it does not run quite smoothly. Also, it falls in hard cubes, squares, and triangles, which again give one the impression of a creaking sound, because of the association with wood. 'Each dull blunt wooden stalactite of rain creaks, hardened by the light'—in the early dawn long raindrops are transformed by the light, until they have the light's own quality of hardness; also they have the dull and blunt and tasteless quality of wood: as they move in

---

[1] Published by Scribner's.

the wind they seem to creak",[1] and so on. Miss Sitwell has justified her poem as an accurate description of her impressions of the early morning: and also illustrated the fact that poetry, even when it is not very good, can convey impressions of sights and sounds far more forcefully than the most painstaking prose: a fact which can also be verified by comparing the description of nature in Hopkins's early journals with those in his poems. The first stanza of *Hurrahing in Harvest*:

"Summer ends now; now, barbarous in beauty, the
    stooks arise
Around; up above, what wind-walks! what lovely
    behaviour
Of silk-sack clouds! has wilder, wilful-wavier
Meal-drift moulded ever and melted across skies?"

is worth all the painstaking prose description of clouds which he laboured at as a young man.

"April 21. We have had other such afternoons, one to-day: the sky a beautiful grained blue, silky lingering clouds in flat-bottomed loaves, others a little browner in ropes or in burly-shouldered ridges swanny and lustrous, more in the zenith stray packs of a sort of violet paleness. White-rose cloud formed fast, not in the same density—some caked and swimming in a wan whiteness, the rest soaked with the blue and like the leaf of a flower held against the light and diapered out by the worm or veining of deeper blue, between rosette and rosette. Later moulding, which brought rain; in perspective it was vaulted in very regular ribs with fretting between; but these are not ribs; they are 'wracking' install

[1] *Poetry and Criticism.* The Hogarth Press.

made of these two realities—the frets, which are scarves of rotten cloud bellying upwards and drooping at their ends, and shaded darkest at the brow or tropic where they double to the eye, and the whiter field of sky showing between: the illusion looking down the 'waggon' is complete. These swaths of fretted cloud move in rank, not in file."[1]

In this passage by dint of mentioning painstakingly all the comparisons suggested to him by the sky of the day he has tried to clamp down, so to speak, the particular quality of the sight which nevertheless has escaped him, and flown off, leaving the description nothing more than a fine piece of empty virtuosity. The poem on the other hand gives, so to speak, the very heart of the impression.

Miss Sitwell uses synaesthesia as a result of what seems to have been a deliberate intellectual resolution. *Aubade* is a poem completely lacking in sensuousness. Hopkins has recourse to it spontaneously and without deliberation: in his poetry it is a consequence of the acute and poignant nature of his sensual experience. As soon as one sense is set alight the rest are similarly affected. Father Lahey mentions an instance of what I take to be Hopkins's extreme sensual sensitiveness which occurs in Hopkins's diary: "as I came in from a stroll with Mr Purbeck he told me Hügel had said the scarlet and rose colour of flamingoes was found to be due to a fine copper powder on their feathers. As he said this I tasted brass in my mouth".

[1] *Life*, by G. F. Lahey, published by the Oxford University Press.

Keats rarely if ever transfers the experience of one sense to that of another. (Hopkins is not however unique among mid-nineteenth-century poets in his use of synaesthesia, for it is a device frequently employed by Swinburne.) It is also true that Keats rarely is content to appeal to only one sense. In such a passage as

"Anon his heart revives; her vespers done,
 Of all its wreathed pearls her hair she frees,
 Unclasps her warmed jewels one by one;
 Loosens her fragrant bodice",

sight, touch and smell are involved. Keats's sensuousness is, so to speak, more lush and less poignant than Hopkins's: but not less remarkable.

In a letter that he sent to Patmore in 1887 Hopkins remarks that Keats's poetry was at every turn abandoning itself to an unmanly and enervating luxury: evidently he felt with Matthew Arnold that Keats's preoccupation with sensual things was in some way unworthy. It may be deduced from this that Hopkins would not have been wholly satisfied with the sensual element in his own poetry.

It seems likely that his aim was always to stiffen and restrict a muse which, left to itself, might have produced poetry characterised by the softness, the richness, the abundance and, so to speak, the fleshiness of *Endymion*. As things are, there is a very great difference between the kind of poetry which Keats wrote and the kind which Hopkins wrote: but possibly the difference is due in some degree to Hopkins's awareness of a potential likeness. His temperament was such that at times he must have been as much tempted as Keats was to give himself up to an "unmanly and enervating luxury".

Hopkins in his poetry does not give himself up to anything at all: it would be difficult to imagine a less passive poet. His poetry is not less rich than that of Keats: but it is more laboured, more descriptive and more self-conscious. There is never any suggestion in his work that he is yielding himself up to any kind of external inspiration: he is always at the helm himself and as fully conscious as possible of what he is doing. There were times, no doubt, when he would have wished to feel himself transported, carried along almost in spite of himself, as other poets seem to have been, as, according to Mr Irving Babbitt, it was the ambition of all romantic poets to be: but from the sonnet in which he complains to Bridges that he wants

"the one rapture of an inspiration",

it appears that he would never think of this inspiration as a power which acts almost independently of the poet's own faculties, which makes the poet into a merely passive instrument: it is nothing more nor less than the "sire" of a "muse" which has the poet's mind for mother. Inspiration is only the beginning: there is a great deal still to be done after the moment of conception.

"Nine months she then, nay years, nine years she long
Within her wears, bears, cares and moulds the same:
The widow of an insight lost she lives, with aim
Now known, and hand at work now never wrong."

He does not think of the inspiration even when it is at its height as relieving the poet of all responsibility: it is essential, but it is very far indeed from being all-sufficient.

The craving for the spontaneous, the natural, the unforced, which Hopkins expresses in this sonnet is related to his love of things "wild". His co-religionist, Von Hügel, once said that the kind of life which should be aimed at was one in which periods of "variety, up to the verge of dissipation" alternating with times of "recollection, up to the verge of emptiness", create a kind of "fruitful tension". Hopkins seems from his poetry to have striven toward just such a sense of spiritual well-being as Von Hügel's recipe was intended to produce: but the periods of "recollection up to the verge of emptiness" were far too frequent for mental comfort. It is evident from the sonnet under consideration that it is not only his muse but his soul which needs some kind of external stimulus, needs to be spurred into spontaneity and abundance of expression. He is tired of living and writing only by his own efforts, without the consciousness of being aided by grace in one field or inspiration in the other: tired of making do with the least possible degree of spiritual assurance and of creative power:

"O then if in my lagging lines you miss
   The roll, the rise, the carol, the creation,
   My winter world, that scarcely breathes that bliss
   Now, yields you, with some sighs, our explanation."

"Winter world" suggests trees, stripped of their leaves and empty of birds, lovely, but with the bare structural beauty which is repugnant to the poet in his present mood. "With some sighs" is an ambiguity in Mr Empson's sense: it may mean either "together with some sighs" or "by means of some sighs". In either case the last line of the sonnet conveys, almost onomatopeically, a strong sense of the difficulty which his muse has in producing even a few scanty words. The sonnet goes in a diminuendo down to the last flat dull word "explanation".

This sonnet shews clearly enough that it was possible for Hopkins to write a poem which was inspired—in the sense that it turned out to be a good poem—at the times when he felt himself most lacking in the vitality and the spontaneity and the insight which are usually described as the results of inspiration. Encouraging Patmore to write the poem in which he had intended to celebrate the Blessed Virgin, Hopkins says: "You wait for your thoughts voluntary to move harmonious numbers: that is nature's way: possibly (for I am not sure of it) the best for natural excellence: but this was to be an act of devotion, of religion; perhaps a strain against nature in the beginning will be the best prospered in the end". His own power of writing poetry which, though it seems not to have originated in any kind of creative ecstasy, is yet thoroughly organic, is one of his most remarkable qualities. The "strain against nature" was certainly prospered in his poetry; we cannot judge what effect the strain may have had on the poet, but evidently it is likely to have been exceptionally fatiguing. His poetry often suggests, I think, that he is, if it is not paradoxical, going beyond his natural resources. If grace aids him, however, it does not do so in such a way as to make hard things easy for him: it only makes them possible. It is his strength in weakness, his power of controlling and ordering his sadness at the moment when it threatens to overwhelm him which gives his poetry the sharp edge, the "temper" as he himself calls it, the "terrible pathos" as it was described by his friend Dixon, which is present above all in the terrible sonnets, *The Windhover* and *Spelt from Sibyl's Leaves*. Extremely sensitive, extremely vulnerable, extremely soft, he is also extreme in his powers of self-control and endurance. His poetry for all its pathos has a much greater virility than that of most of the poets who make play with manliness and bluffness and vigour. It was at this kind of virility that Keats was aiming, to judge from the letters and the second version of *Hyperion*. His very sensuousness might have served, as that of Hopkins did, to increase his capacity for suffering and so his scope for exercising the virile virtues of patience and self-control. A mature Keats would, it seems likely, have had much in common with Hopkins: like him, he would have had two strings to his bow: he would have excelled not only in softness and depth of colour, but in sharpness of outline and symmetry. In other words he would have united, as Hopkins did, the qualities generally ascribed to romantic poets with those said to be characteristic of the classical.

IV

It seems to have been Hopkins's fate to combine in his poetry characteristics which have been treated as incompatible with one another, belonging to categories which are directly opposed. Mr Graves, in the essay from which I have already quoted, takes Keats as a type of the poet who depends largely upon his power of appealing to the senses not only of sight but of touch, taste and hearing; and Shelley as an example of the disembodied spirit who for precise and particularised sensations substitutes a vague feeling of the motion behind all things. Keats's poetry is "tactile, visile, audile, and so on"; Shelley's is motile. Mr Graves connects this fact with the other fact that Keats's poetry is in a manner of speaking concrete, while Shelley's is ethereal—he prefers scenery as it is reflected in water to scenery as it is actually, because it is one remove further from what is actually seen and heard and grasped: and so on. But Hopkins's poetry, while it is not less "tactile, visile and audile" than that of Keats, is also as motile as that of Shelley. There is the difference that while Shelley sees everything in Nature as drifting in a state of lazy flux, Hopkins sees it as animated by a most violently dynamic force. He sees columns falling over each other, flames pushing up, leaves shooting out. The sky to him is never a painted cloth; it is full of colours hurrying to replace each other.

"The descending blue; that blue is all in a rush
With richness—"

In his early prose he describes an April sky as "like clean oil but just as full of colour, shaken over with slanted flashing 'travellers' all in flight, stepping one behind the other, their edges tossed with bright as if white napkins were thrown up in the sun but not quite at the same moment, so that they were all in a scale down the air, falling one after the other to the ground" (Lahey, p. 163). At night he sees in the skies

"Grey lawns cold where gold, where quickgold lies!
Wind-beat whitebeam! airy abeles set on a flare!
Flake-doves sent floating forth at a farmyard scare."

He sees events in a series, as in the lines from the *Wreck of the Deutschland* in which he describes Christ as

"The heaven-flung heart-fleshed, maiden-furled
Miracle-in-Mary-of-flame..."

The dynamic nature of his imagery makes the theme "That Nature is a Heraclitean Fire" congenial to him: it is with extreme relish that he describes "Million-fuelèd nature's bonfire".

"Cloud-puffball, torn tufts, tossed pillows ǀ flaunt
forth, then chevy on an air-
built thoroughfare: heaven-roysterers, in gay-
gangs ǀ they throng; they glitter in marches.

Down roughcast, down dazzling whitewash, | when-
    ever an elm arches,
Shivelights and shadowtackle in long lashes | lace,
    lance, and pair.
Delightfully the bright wind boisterous | ropes,
    wrestles, beats earth bare
Of yestertempest's creases; in pool and rut peel
    parches
Squandering ooze to squeezed | dough, crust, dust;
    stanches, starches
Squadroned masks and manmarks | treadmire toil
    there
Footfretted in it. Million-fuelèd |, nature's bonfire
    burns on.
But quench her bonniest, dearest | to her, her
    clearest-selvèd spark
Man, how fast his firedint, | his mark on mind, is
    gone!'"

The flux itself gives him no sensation of distress; on
the contrary he is thoroughly at home in a world
where everything is rushing to and fro in a transport
of wild activity. No accent of distress comes into
the poem until he suggests to himself the thought
that when man and mind fall out of this mad chase
there is no other performer to succeed them. It is
perhaps worth noting as symptomatic of the pleasure
which he takes in movement and his dread and dislike of immobility, that the stone to which he
compares man's soul, the stone which signifies per-
manence, hardness, indestructibility is a diamond—
a stone which by its brilliance, its attraction for
light, however still it may be held, has still a kind of
mobility, winking in the sun, darting its rays now in

one direction and now in another. The poem begins
with imagery which represents and excites movement on a grand scale: it ends with motion which is
on a very small scale, but still with motion.

"This Jack, joke, poor potsherd, | patch, matchwood,
    immortal diamond,
  Is immortal diamond."

The very sound of "diamond" leaves the reader
with the impression of the stone wincing in the light
and dazzling the eye: immortal, but not immobile:
an indestructible lump of shivering light. If the
poem had ended in an image which suggested a
complete standstill it would in all likelihood have
indicated that the poet's mood had become one of
extreme sadness; as in *Spelt from Sibyl's Leaves*
where the end of the pictured movement brings the
poet's terror to its climax. *The Windhover*, like the
Heraclitean poem, is interesting in this connection:
it ends with an image which represents movement
on a very small scale: that of the ash-fire which can
only quiver and dissolve, forfeiting its being piece
by piece. This image, unlike the diamond, conveys
the impression that it was suggested to the poet by
the most extreme distress: but that is partly because
the activity of the fire is contrasted with the movements of the kestrel who has all the sky for his play-
ground: and it does not conflict with what I have
said about the satisfaction which Hopkins derives
from any kind of movement, because it seems
very likely that the distress which Hopkins has

expressed in *The Windhover* was greater than he realised: he meant the quivering of the ash-fire to symbolise an activity which was as pleasant to Christ, and therefore to the performer, as the wheeling of the kestrel could be: he thought that he had reconciled himself to the fact that he could do nothing but suffer while the bird had only to indulge his instincts, to strike off splendour from his wings and at the same time please his Maker: it is only the reader who realises that Hopkins's

"Fall, gall themselves and gash gold-vermilion"

shews him to be in a state of mind in which resignation brings with it no consolation, a state of mind which is only saved from being one of utter defeat by the fact that he is still able to exercise his will, and in order to acquiesce deliberately in the misery designed for him at the moment. Hopkins's poetry goes directly against Mr Graves's suggestion that "motile" imagery proceeds as a rule from a poet who lives, to quote a line from Chapman,

"rather without the body than within",

for Hopkins is entrenched very firmly behind his five senses. Mr Empson has suggested that it is possible that dynamic imagery characterises a poet who likes to give himself up to some external force—in Hopkins's case, the Church: in Shelley's it would be, I suppose, the Cause of Mankind, and so on. But I doubt whether either of these theories will be felt to be satisfactory. Before proceeding to any generalisation of this kind it would be necessary to make some very fine distinctions. There are, for example, many different ways of being preoccupied with movement. There may be many varieties of "motile" imagery. Also it is rare to find a poet whose imagery is consistently dynamic or consistently static.

From such a passage as the following one would deduce that Wordsworth, for example, was a poet who loved the dynamic, loved the sense of being carried away, rather as Shelley did.

> " . . . oftentimes
> When we had given our bodies to the wind,
> And all the shadowy banks on either side
> Came sweeping through the darkness, spinning still
> The rapid line of motion, then at once
> Have I, reclining back upon my heels,
> Stopped short; yet still the solitary cliffs
> Wheeled by me—even as if the earth had rolled
> With visible motion her diurnal round!
> Behind me did they stretch in solemn train,
> Feebler and feebler, and I stood and watched
> Till all was tranquil as a dreamless sleep."

Although it would be equally possible to make the deduction that Wordsworth likes the return to repose after exertion more than the exertion itself. His poetry is in any case not consistent in this respect; in the passage above, the sight of the earth rolling

> "with visible motion her diurnal round"

is associated with pleasure, though no doubt it is pleasure which is tempered with awe. In the poem called *A Slumber did my Spirit Seal* the movement of the earth on its diurnal course becomes a symbol of remorseless fate or remorseless time: it is like a wheel which will not stop moving, whatever catastrophe may have befallen its passengers. Lucy, who may once have felt as the young Wordsworth did, that she was the centre of the world, that if it revolved it revolved round her, is now as inert and inconsiderable as any of the pieces of wood and stone which decorate the earth's surface.

> "No motion has she now, no force;
>   She neither hears nor sees,
>   Rolled round in earth's diurnal course
>   With rocks, and stones, and trees."

In one mood motion is to Wordsworth a symbol of pleasure: in another of pain: motile imagery is not more characteristic of him than static imagery.

The same is true, I think, of Milton. Judging from the description of Mulciber's fall from heaven

>   "thrown by angry Jove
> Sheer o'er the crystal battlements: from morn
> To noon he fell, from noon to dewy eve.
> A summer's day: and with the setting sun
> Dropped from the zenith like a falling star
> On Lemnos th' Aegean isle",

one would say that his imagery was extremely dynamic: but the imagery of most of his work would not provoke the reader to consider the question of static or dynamic at all. There are, I think, very few poets whose imagery is consistently one or the other, or who seem to have a marked predilection for either movement or stasis. Shelley's love of the drifting:

> "My soul is an enchanted boat
> Which, like a sleeping swan doth float
> Upon the silver waves of thy sweet singing";

and flying:

> "On the brink of the night and the morning
> My coursers are wont to respire
> But the Earth has just whispered a warning
> That their flight must be swifter than fire";

is striking: and there is no doubt that delight in his poetry is usually connected with movement—the imagery of the last act of the *Prometheus Unbound* rushes at a delirious rate, with intervals of languorous floating; and Hopkins's love of movement is equally striking, different as it is from Shelley's. Hopkins loves any kind of movement, not only the effortless movement of drifting and flying. The movement which is the product not of delirium but of normal energy is his favourite symbol of delight. Yeats has suggested that the image most characteristic of Shelley is that of a boat drifting down a river between high hills. The image most characteristic of Hopkins is that of a bird—the Windhover or the stormfowl of the Purcell sonnet—striking off beauty from its plumage as it wheels and turns, intent only on exercising the faculties with which it is endowed.

There is little to be said, I think, in favour of attempting to classify poets according to the motile or static nature of the imagery which they use:

because the consistency of Hopkins in this respect is singular. The only poet I can think of whose work shews an equally consistent devotion to one kind of imagery is Valéry, whose imagery is as markedly static as that of Hopkins is dynamic. Hopkins's imagery rushes like a river: Valéry's images are succinct and detached, rarely merging into each other, as Hopkins's almost always do—

"self-wrung, self-strung, sheathe- and shelterless",

for instance. Valéry might have taken for his motto Gide's maxim, "ne jamais profiter de l'impétus acquise". Hopkins's images are like pailfulls of water poured into a fast stream; Valéry's are the single detached blows of a man chipping at a block of stone. As Hopkins is interested most in things which are in motion, creatures which are exercising all their energies, Valéry is most attracted by things in equilibrium: the sycamore held by the foot, grasped by the dead who lie underneath its roots and yet drawn towards the sky, in the poem *Au Platane*: or the palm, of which he writes

> "Admire comme elle vibre
> Et comme une lente fibre
> Qui divise le moment,
> Départage sans mystère
> L'attirance de la terre
> Et le poids du firmament!"[1]

Again, while Hopkins is interested in action, in progress, it is the moment just before and the

[1] *Charmes*, Published by the Librairie Gallimard, Editions de la Nouvelle Revue Francaise.

moment just after action which concerns Valéry. *Les Pas* shews his delight in the tautness of expectancy which precedes action:

> "ne hâte pas cet acte tendre
> Douceur d'être et de n'être pas."

The *Ode Secrète* shews his delight in the return to equilibrium as, after violent exertion, the body of the hero returns to repose, outstretched on the grass

> "Chute superbe, fin si douce
> Oubli des luttes, quel délice
> Que d'étendre à même la mousse
> Après la danse, le corps lisse."

In other words, Hopkins, if he is writing a poem about the destruction of Sodom and Gomorrah would be likely to concentrate on the overthrow of the cities: Valéry on the incident of Lot's wife turning into a pillar of salt. Activity is distasteful to him and he hates the turmoil which Hopkins loves. In the poem *La Pythie* one feels that it is with great relief that he leaves the foaming prophetess and comes to describe the result of her torments. Hopkins likes turmoil; in the *Wreck of the Deutschland* it is evident that he is quite at ease in the storm.

The antithesis is exceptionally near to being complete. It might be true to say that the antithesis is maintained in the poets' attitudes to their respective selves: Valéry hates to be carried away; he likes to stand still, like Narcissus, plumbing the depths of his   "inépuisable Moi", or like the speaker in *Le Cimetière Marin*,

"O pour moi seul, à moi seul, en moi-même,
Auprès d'un cœur, aux sources du poème,
Entre le vide et l'événement pur,
J'attends l'écho de ma grandeur interne
Amère, sombre et sonore citerne
Sonnant dans l'âme un creux toujours futur."

If Hopkins is made more than usually conscious of his own identity as separate from the rest of the creation, it causes him pain.

"I am gall, I am heartburn. God's most deep decree
Bitter would have me taste: my taste was me;
Bones built in me, flesh filled, blood brimmed the curse."

The difference between Valéry's and Hopkins's attitudes to their own selves is possibly connected with the fact that Hopkins is a Christian and so dreads the feeling of being separated from God—as represented by his creation. But what deduction is to be made from the other features of the antithesis I do not know: except that Hopkins's love of the organic may be connected with the organic nature of his own poetry. Hopkins's poems, at their best, seem to have grown like plants. Valéry's, even at their best, have an air of being contrived, built up piece by piece like the flower which the Chinese make out of pieces of cornelian and rock amethyst. But it would be very dangerous to take this deduction any further: all organic poetry does not bear witness to an unusual love of movement in the poet nor is it true that all poetry of which the imagery is static gives as Valéry's does the impression of being contrived, of being an imitation more precious perhaps than the original itself, but still not the "real thing".

V

Temperamentally Hopkins had more in common with Keats than with any other nineteenth-century poet, I think: but his work suggests that he had also a true, though slight affinity with Wordsworth. His likeness to Keats is largely potential and a matter of conjecture: such affinity as he has with Wordsworth comes out quite clearly in his work as it stands. The degree of affinity between Hopkins and a poet described habitually and not unjustly as the supreme Romantic and the poet of the unconscious and so on could not be great: but it is enough to make a comparison instructive, even if, as is here the case, it brings to light more points of dissimilarity than of likeness. Hopkins's poetry has many more different strains in it than Wordsworth's has: so much is evident at the start. As Coleridge pointed out, Wordsworth trades constantly and almost exclusively on involuntary and in a sense irrational associations of ideas and emotions—it was this which made his poetry difficult for such a mind as Jeffrey's, which was accustomed to strict logical sequence. In *The Thorn*, for instance, unless the tree and the mad mother are felt instinctively to be in close relationship the poem must strike the reader as obscure in the extreme: and in this difficulty logic will not be of much help. Hopkins on the other hand makes great play with logical associations; his poetry appeals as much to the unconscious as Wordsworth's does; but it also involves the conscious. It has been said by one critic that Wordsworth's poetry is like water: it is so clear that a careless observer is apt to be misled into thinking that there is nothing in it. Hopkins's poetry on the other hand is so highly coloured that it might almost strike a distrustful reader as likely to prove an unwholesome drink. It is partly that much more of the content of Hopkins's poetry is on the surface. If Wordsworth's poetry is like clear water, it is like the clear water of a well which has nevertheless a good deal of mud (by calling it mud I do not mean to suggest that it is bad) at the bottom: "the cult of simplicity moved its complexity back into the sub-conscious, poisoned only the sources of thought in the high bogs of the mountain", says Mr Empson. Hopkins's complexity is not repressed; it is on the surface and plain for all the world to see.

Goethe in his *Poetry and Life* says, surprisingly to a modern ear, that the grandest and most essential part of poetry is that which can be conveyed in a prose paraphrase. No doubt Goethe exaggerated grossly: but the part in question is possibly important enough to justify one in saying that there is a genuine affinity between Wordsworth and Hopkins on the ground that there is a striking likeness to Wordsworth in the prose statements of some of Hopkins's poems. From these it would become evident that Hopkins and Wordsworth shared the belief that it is possible to come to a very strong sense of the divine presence through those aspects of nature which present themselves to the eye and ear. At the outset there is of course the difference that while Wordsworth apprehends in Nature a deity who is omnipresent, and to some extent vague, merely

> "A presence that disturbs me with the joy
> Of elevated thoughts",

Hopkins seems actually to obtain from Nature a sense of the presence of one or other of the persons of the Trinity. I think this makes his pantheistic poems appear superficially at any rate stranger and more far-fetched than those of Wordsworth; perhaps simply because Wordsworth's attitude has become so much more familiar to us. Stupidly, perhaps, we do not expect to find a Jesuit poet seeing God in Nature. St John of the Cross liked to look out of his window on a pleasant landscape, as a concession to the flesh; but when he wished to see God he shut his eyes. It must be remembered, however, that Hopkins was not specially a mystic and probably not a saint. He was a devout Christian and a man of extreme intellectual scrupulousness who aimed at reconciling what he knew of the natural world with what he knew and believed of the spiritual; it was not unadvisedly that I compared him to von Hügel. In a rational Christianity the body must play a considerable part; and Hopkins is not ashamed of allowing his senses to provide him with ways of approach to God: though it is true that he seems to think it necessary to justify his belief that God is visible and audible in Nature. Some of the verses of the *Wreck of the Deutschland* suggest that the specifically Christian raptures which, in his own experience, Nature sometimes affords, date from the time of Christ's Incarnation. Since he was in the world the whole universe has been unified, has become, so to speak, a single huge relic.

The raptures which Nature sometimes confers on Hopkins are not achieved as effortlessly as those of Wordsworth are: Wordsworth coolly and effortlessly steps

"into a sort of oneness":

he attains his goal by sheer passivity. Hopkins on the other hand is all the time struggling and straining to arrive at the assurance of the divine presence which he longs for. This is seen very clearly in *Hurrahing in Harvest* where as he walks he lifts up, lifts up heart, eyes

"Down all that glory in the heavens to glean our Saviour."

"To glean": Hopkins's ecstasy is to some extent the result of a mental process, a collecting and piecing together of the traces which Christ has left in the world in which he lives. Wordsworth is blamed by Mr Irving Babbitt for substituting the ecstasies to be obtained from the 'subrational' and the 'subconscious' for those in which reason and divine grace co-operate: on those grounds he should think well of Hopkins.

Again, for all the reverence in which he holds Nature Wordsworth is much bolder in his demands than Hopkins dares to be. If Wordsworth suddenly finds that he has no spiritual joy in Nature he takes it for granted that the fault is his own; given that his eye is clear and his mind is open, then certainly the sense of oneness will come. Hopkins on the other hand is conscious that he must await the divine pleasure; that he cannot merely by his own efforts obtain the assurance which he wants.

"I kiss my hand
  To the stars, lovely-asunder
  Starlight, wafting him out of it; and
  Glow, glory in thunder;
  Kiss my hand to the dappled-with-damson-west:
  Since, though he is under the world's splendour
    and wonder,
  His mystery must be instressed, stressed;
  For I greet him the days I meet him, and bless
    when I understand."

The gesture of "kissing the hand" is made to persons who are far away, or at least out of reach; Hopkins is very conscious of the distance at which he must keep himself: the friendship which may exist between the human and the divine must never lapse into familiarity.

The poems in which Hopkins is preoccupied with

the theme of God's presence in Nature are not very numerous. They are, besides those already mentioned, *God's Grandeur*, in which he attributes the loneliness of Nature's everyday self to the Holy Spirit who broods over the world with "warm breast and with ah! bright wings"; *The Starlight Night* and *Spring* in which he suggests that the charm of Nature's wildness dates from the days before man had sinned, that it is a remnant of the freshness of that primitive Eden in which God walked. But there are others which for a different reason invite comparison with Wordsworth. Wordsworth says, in the preface to the *Lyrical Ballads*, that it was his aim in some of his poems to "choose incidents from common life and make them interesting by tracing in them the primary laws of our nature"; and so, curiously enough, we have Wordsworth, in some ways the most egotistical of poets, entering into the feelings of little girls feeding lambs, mothers who have lost their sons, wives deserted by their husbands, peasants living in cities as exiles from their own country. Wordsworth's power of sympathy is of a kind that might well draw strictures from Mr Irving Babbitt. It is not by grace or anything like it that he is enabled to step into the shoes of poor Susan or afflicted Margaret: the process of tracing in their actions the primary laws in our nature is not an intellectual one. He arrives at sympathy with them by falling back on a sort of blood-bond which links the whole human race together. If he had been a contemporary of our own, Wordsworth would very likely have been denounced by Mr Wyndham Lewis for conniving at the return to the Primitive which was said three or four years ago to be making havoc in our society. As it was he was denounced as a barbarian by Peacock in his *Four Ages of Poetry*. "While the historian and philosopher are advancing and accelerating the progress of knowledge, the poet is wallowing in the rubbish of departed ignorance, and raking up the ashes of dead savages to find gewgaws and rattles for the grown babies of the age."

There is little in Hopkins's poetry which the most inveterate anti-romantic would think it his duty to denounce as primitive or barbarian or infantile; he is a singularly mature and, in a good sense of the adjective, a singularly conscious poet: but the little group of poems in which he tried to enter sympathetically into the hearts of other human beings to trace the primary laws of human nature working in incidents chosen from his everyday experience contains several which are inferior to the rest of his own poetry and very inferior to most of Wordsworth's works which deal with similar themes. It looks as though the workings of a subrational kind of sympathy can on occasion make better poetry than those of a sympathy which is the result of intellectual labour and aspiration after divine grace.

The poems of Hopkins to which I refer were most of them written at one time: they are *The Bugler's First Communion*, *Felix Randal*, *Brothers*, *The Handsome Heart* and the poem which though unfinished is by far the best of the group, with the exception of *Spring and Fall, On the Portrait of Two Beautiful Young People*. The task which Hopkins sets before him is not, it must be admitted, as simple as Wordsworth's. Usually his aim is not merely to trace the primary laws of human nature but to trace them in relation to, or as they are under the influence of, divine grace. *The Bugler's First Communion* is praised by one critic as "unsurpassed in its sense of the beauty of adolescence". The sense of the beauty of adolescence was certainly part of what Hopkins wished to convey: in all these poems he deals with a particular incident which has a general import. But I must admit that this particular poem leaves me very uncomfortable. Though it contains many felicitous lines and phrases,

"dress his days to a dexterous and starlight order",

or   "that brow and bead of being",

for example, it is as a whole discordant and somehow false.

Hopkins is as minutely and unnecessarily circumstantial in his description of the incident as Wordsworth in the description of the old sea-captain who tells the story of the mad mother. He tells us that the boy comes from a barrack, which is over the hill there: that his father is English and his mother Irish (here the metaphysical poet who is always present in Hopkins lifts his head and tries to rationalise the introduction of this not very significant piece of information by venturing a conjecture as to the probable effects of this mixture of nationality on

(48)

the boy's character). The next verse reads as though Hopkins were trying to prolong the excitement which he felt when the incident occurred.

"This very very day came down to us after a boon
    he on
  My late being there begged of me, overflowing
  Boon in my bestowing,
  Came, I say, this day to it—to a First Communion."

But the flatness of the second line suggests that his attempt to recapture the sensation has failed.

"Here he knelt then in regimental red.
  Forth Christ from cupboard fetched, how fain I of
    feet
  To his youngster take his treat!
  Low-latched in leaf-light housel his too huge god-
    head."

In the third verse the fact that the boy was in uniform is given a portentous air which is scarcely justified: the emotion which it presumably inspired in the poet is not reproduced in the reader. The would-be directness and simplicity of "youngster" and "treat" reach the reader as a forced heartiness: and in poetry so sophisticated as that of Hopkins the very picture given here of the way in which Christ is present in the wafer is odd and to me disagreeable. It is not the fact that they contain doctrine of Transubstantiation which makes these lines repugnant; there is nothing repugnant in St Thomas Aquinas's *Rythmus ad SS. Sacramentum*, "Adoro te supplex latens deitas", nor in Hopkins's translation of it. It is, I think, the unsuccessful attempt at childlike simplicity in the description of the doctrine—Christ dwelling in the wafer as in a little house of which the door is locked—which repels. The sham heartiness of which I have spoken reappears in "slips of soldiery"; and the apparently unconscious sensuousness of

> "Limber liquid youth, that to all I teach
>   Yields tender as a pushed peach",

and

> "Fresh youth fretted in a bloomfall all portending
>   That sweet's sweeter ending",

jars in a poem which contains praises of chastity (if this is a fault, it is one which is constantly occurring in Crashaw's work; but faults which are not grave in Crashaw's work may be so in that of Hopkins, which is much more conscious and sophisticated), besides suggesting that the Deity is a kind of ogre, waiting to swallow-up-alive.

Destructive criticism of this kind is not very valuable; perhaps all that needs to be said is that Hopkins's attempt at simplicity and directness fails; the poem recovers when he is beginning to consider his own complicated reactions to the incident, the mixture of faith and misgiving with which he looks forward to the child's future:

> "Recorded only, I have put my lips on pleas
>   Would brandle adamantine heaven with ride and
>   jar, did Prayer go disregarded;
>   Forward-like, but however, and like favourable
>   heaven heard these."

If *The Bugler's First Communion* fails in simplicity *Felix Randal*, though a much better poem, fails to some extent in sympathy. On the other hand, against these failures there may be set two great successes: the now well-known *Spring and Fall: to a Young Child* is a successful poem of the same kind as *The Bugler's First Communion*: *On the Portrait of Two Beautiful Young People* would if finished have been a great poem and it is one of which the mainspring is that sympathy with other and remote human microcosms which in *Felix Randal* seems a little forced and artificial. In *Spring and Fall* Hopkins traces such of the "primary laws of human nature" as are at work in the figure of a young child crying at the sight of a golden grove whose trees are growing bare and leafless. He does not fall back on a sort of racial sympathy in his effort to enter into the child's mind, as Wordsworth does in *Alice Fell* and *Barbara Lewthwaite*: he is all the while a person quite separate from the child, made remote from her by his age and experience and calling, although like her he is one of the doomed human race whose fate is foreshadowed in that of the trees. The process by which he arrives at the solution of the question—what is she grieving for?—is largely an intellectual one; he uses the subtlety and shews the insight of a good confessor. Tenderness in this poem as in all Hopkins's best poems, is well under control; here it is subordinated to the impulse towards unsparing candour—he will not leave the child in ignorance, much as he would perhaps like to do so—; and to the free play of the intellect, which hovers round the slight, mysterious incident, at last to pounce and link it up with the history and the future of the whole human race. There is no false simplicity here, no spurts of sentimentality nor excessive sensuousness; the poem is everything which *The Bugler's First Communion* might have been and was not.

Felix Randal is another poem in which the poet reminds the reader that he is a priest. But it is a poem which lacks entirely the sane, solemn tenderness of *Spring and Fall*. The loose, almost uncontrolled rhythm and the exaggerated phraseology,

"When thou at the random grim forge, powerful amidst peers,
    Didst fettle for the great grey drayhorse his bright and battering sandal",

alike suggest that the poet is abandoning himself to an unchecked emotionalism over which the intellect exercises no censorship. There is a suggestion too that by force of will he is working himself up to a pitch of grief for Felix Randal which normally he would not reach.

"This seeing the sick endears them to us, us too it endears.
  My tongue had taught thee comfort, touch had quenched thy tears,
  Thy tears that touched my heart, child, Felix, poor Felix Randal."

That is a verse which seems to me to read as though the poet were encouraging his emotions to take more sway over him than they would normally: he is trying by repeating the man's name, by rehearsing the circumstances of his illness to work himself up to a frenzy of compassion. Finally he has recourse to the thought of the heedlessness of his coming death which characterised the blacksmith Randal in his prime; and the poem ends with a clangorous reconstruction of the smith at work at his forge; a reconstruction which by force of contrast with the picture of the wasted invalid, now a corpse, which Hopkins has in his mind, ought to be extremely moving. But the poet's intention is too overt; and the reader, if I am to speak for myself, recoils before so evident an attack on his tender feelings: his tears retreat like the eyes of the snail

"into the shelly caverns of his head."

If *Spring and Fall* and *Felix Randal* were to be paraphrased, there would be no more reason to think *Felix Randal* an unsuccessful poem than to think *Spring and Fall* so: but as it stands, considered as an organic whole, *Felix Randal* fails, though it is difficult to say why, and the rather peevish fault-finding in which I have been indulging does not make clear why it should be so. It seems that the motion of accepting or rejecting a poem comes from the very quick of the will; it is rarely possible to give a wholly satisfactory account of one's reasons for doing one or the other.

The unfinished poem called *On the Portrait of Two Beautiful Young People* has verses which are greater than anything else in Hopkins's Wordsworthian poems; and which, in kind at any rate, if not in achievement, are greater than most of Wordsworth's own Poems of the Affections. Hopkins in this poem evokes a sense of the immense consequences attendant upon each act of the human will, and of the pitiableness of the best-equipped assemblage of human powers in face of the hostile forces, which invite comparison with the effect of a Shakespearean tragedy. In this poem Hopkins's attitude as priest and theologian stand him in good stead; his poetry has, I think, on that account, a variety and richness which is absent as a rule from Wordsworth. I include this poem amongst the Wordsworthian ones because it is, like *Felix Randal*, an exercise, so to speak, in sympathy; but though Felix Randal was known to him and of these two young people he knows nothing, his conjectures as to their character and destiny stir in him a far deeper solicitude than did the death of his blacksmith penitent. His pity for and fear for the whole of humanity is wakened by these two portraits; they symbolise for him the human race as perhaps the well-known figure of Felix Randal could not; and yet they do not lose their own individuality, and his feeling for them is in no way weakened by being diffused over the whole of mankind. It is characteristic of Hopkins, I think, that it is in this poem in which he is, as he says, "straining his heart beyond his ken", that he identifies himself the most completely with other human beings: he was not nearly direct enough and simple enough to make his greatest poetry out of incidents drawn from actual life; the more scope there was for the free play of the intellect in his poetry, the more at ease he was; Hopkins's mind is much more given to the formal and the abstract than Wordsworth's, and could not easily submit itself to the arbitrariness of actual experience.

As the poem, besides being one of Hopkins's best, is also one of his most obscure, I shall attempt some kind of paraphrase and commentary on it, without pretending to disengage or hint at all the possible meanings.

In the first verse the poet is considering, half in pity, half in awe, the way in which transience is so often a characteristic of beauty and somehow forms part of it.

"O I admire and sorrow! The heart's eye grieves
Discovering you, dark tramplers, tyrant years.
A juice rides rich through bluebells, in vine leaves,
And beauty's dearest veriest vein is tears."

His sorrow is not bitter; it is mingled with wonder, he seems to admit that there may be some satisfactory explanation of the phenomenon, not yet known to him. When he thinks of the way in which the years, the dark tramplers—Yeats's black oxen—spoil human beauty he is sad and indignant. But in the next line there is a suggestion that the dark tramplers may be serving some useful end. Oxen stamping out the sap of bluebells could only be wantonly destructive; but the vine must be trodden deliberately and systematically if it is ever to give up its life-giving juice. What the sap is to the blue-bell and the vine, tears are to beauty: it is sorrow which keeps beauty alive; our grief that it cannot last is part of our love for the beautiful thing.

The image of the vine and bluebell also serves, at any rate for me, to conjure up visual images of the two young people: the bluebell gives us the grace of the sister and the vine the vitality and robustness of the young man.

The word "vein" is one which often recurs in Hopkins's poetry, perhaps on account of his interest in processes; he is always conscious of the strange-ness of the mechanisms by which life is maintained; he seems to have that sense of the strangeness of the world of nature which T. E. Hulme took to be one of the characteristics of the religious mind, which, according to him, is more at home in the geo-metrical and conventional world of the Byzantine artist than in the unruly world of nature. If this is so then Hopkins's attitude is half religious, half irre-ligious—for he is not completely at home in either. But Hulme's definition of the religious attitude is a narrow one and in any case one would not expect it to describe that of Hopkins, because Hulme was concerned to magnify the gulf between the spiritual and the natural which Hopkins wanted to bridge.

To return to the poem; in the next verse Hopkins, with the movement of instinctive deference and admiration which, he says in another poem, is beauty's due, cries out:

"Happy the father, mother of these!"

But he has no sooner said it than he is overtaken by the memory of the instability of all human life and of the pitiful frailty of human goodness. Fear begins to creep in on him. It has been said that it is difficult to see why Hopkins is so very much weighed down by what he thinks was the probable fate of this handsome pair; there seems to have been no reason why he should have been more fearful for them than for anyone else; though his fears for them are made more painful by the pity and admiration excited in him by their beauty. I think that the explanation is partly that at this time Hopkins was in something of the mood which he describes in *Spelt from Sibyl's Leaves*, a mood in which the ideas of right and wrong, black and white, damnation and salvation, dwarf every other consideration. Against this solemn background the youth and beauty of the two creatures who must eventually be parcelled, penned, packed into one or other of the folds, seem something very slight and fluttering: he is painfully conscious that none of this will help them in the realm where right and wrong are the only categories.

"Not that, but thus far, all with frailty, blest
In one fair fall; but, for time's aftercast,
Creatures all heft, hope, hazard, interest."

Aftercast suggests that time is throwing dice: the first throw has been a kind one. But he is terrified by the hazardousness of the future. Hope in this context suggests something very tenuous, something which is not nearly strong enough to counterbalance hazard. It seems likely that the poet was, perhaps unconsciously and certainly irrationally, convinced that the fate of the two young people was evil.

The question with which he begins the next verse is to be accounted for, I think, by the fact that with their picture before his eyes, so fresh and clear and definite, it is difficult to believe that any contingency could alter them or make their beauty a thing of no significance. But reason snatches away the con‑ solation, reminding him that it is only by chance that there is any memorial whatever of their love‑ liness.

"And are they thus? The fine, the fingering beams
   Their young delightful hour do feature down
   That fleeted else like day-dissolvèd dreams
   Or ringlet-race on burling Barrow brown."

It is only by the fine strokes of the painter's tiny brush that their youth is kept alive.

"Bright forelock, cluster that you are
   Of favoured make and mind and health and youth"

in the next verse but one is interesting as suggesting that Hopkins is considering them as part of humanity as a whole, to which they stand in the relation in which a lovely curl stands to the human body. In another poet this trick of considering humanity for a moment as a kind of single huge lump might indicate some sort of bitterness of spirit and it may of course indicate something of the sort in Hopkins, though it seems more likely that it is merely a sign that he is for the moment standing aloof from all things in philosophic abstraction. It is certainly not in any kind of bitterness that he describes the bugler boy as a "brow and bead of being".

The reply to the question:

"Where lies your landmark, seamark, or soul's star?"

ought to bring a note of confidence and reassurance into the poem.

"There's none but truth can stead you. Christ is
    truth."

Only Christ can save them; but then Christ is easily accessible, with arms wide to all men. It is an unreasoning despair, an inescapable foreboding which makes the line as it stands so full of doom. Hopkins somehow suggests that the two young people will not avail themselves of the truth: they will insist on trusting themselves to unstable substitutes and so perish—a suggestion carried on in the next verse.

"There's none but good can bé good, both for you
    And what sways with you, maybe this sweet maid;
    None good but God—a warning wavèd to
    One once that was found wanting when Good
        weighed."

There is no easy way out; no way of avoiding the momentous choice between good and evil on which depends the welfare of the young man and of all who depend on him. "Sways" suggests very powerfully the frailty and instability of their hold on happiness: it is as though they are on the verge of a precipice: movement in one direction means safety, in the other destruction, and they are wavering. There is a hint of the same thing in the verse before, in the phrase "there's none but Christ can stead you", where "stead" is evidently ambiguous, meaning both "be of use to" and "steady". My impression that Hopkins feels that these two, for all their beauty and amiability and good intentions, will make the wrong choice is confirmed by the fact that, looking at them, his mind turns naturally to the instance of the rich young man, who was virtuous and whom Christ loved, and who yet turned away, because he had great possessions.

The next verse is the climax of the poem and perhaps the best single verse in all his work. Here, with as much clarity as compression, he gives his conception of free will and predestination: the lines are calm and almost unemotional: the poet speaks with the air of one enunciating a truth so great that no emotional response to it could be adequate.

"Man lives that list, that leaning in the will
  No wisdom can forecast by gauge or guess,
  That selfless self of self, most strange, most still,
  Fast furled and all foredrawn to No or Yes."

The result of the choice is predestined: man's life follows out the trend of his own will. Although no one can foresee in which direction it inclines the bent is already there, in the very core of his being. The self which chooses is fast furled, it is shut tight, like a bud, but the nature of the flower is pre-ordained. "List and leaning" suggest that he is thinking of the will as a kind of ship, an image which looks back to the "landmark, seamark" of an earlier verse.

After the terrifying impersonality of this reflection it is a relief to turn again to the charming portrait; but the loveliness of the two faces seems this time to throw the poet into deeper despair:

"Your feast of; that most in you earnest eye
May but call on your banes to more carouse.
Worst will the best. What worm was here, we cry,
To have havoc-pocked so, see, the hung-heaven-
  ward boughs?"

He says "may"; but it is clear enough that "will" would better express his feelings about the pair. "Your feast of" is a phrase which it is easy enough for the reader to finish for himself: as it stands it expresses the delicacy, the abundance and the variety of the charms (charms is not the right word, but this was not meant to be said in prose) of the two creatures. The eye, the most spiritual part of the face with its serious intent expression, may only make the victim more tempting to the huge, shadowy, hostile, greedy, shapes of evil of which he conjures up the image by the cryptic Saxon word "banes". "Worst will the best" is what Mr Empson calls an ambiguity. The best will become the worst or the worst, the evil powers, will insist on making the best of humanity its own. It is all summed up in the picture of the blossoming aspiring tree with its natural bent and its natural shape, the order of its boughs, destroyed by the pest. "Worm" in a verse so full of Anglo-Saxon words suggests not only "pest" but "dragon". "Worm" in Anglo-Saxon would have signified some monstrous shape of evil, perhaps the devil himself, the worm who crept into Eden. The picture which the lines call up of the dragon under the tree is not unapt here, for the blossoming tree is a symbol of life and in Christian art of the redemptive power of Christ's cross, and it is against these that the dragon works.

In the last verse Hopkins tries to subdue the tide of pity and fear which is threatening to overwhelm him by the reflection that "corruption was the world's first woe"; the two young people are not the first and will not be the last to be destroyed by evil; a reflection which is more likely to aggravate his grief than to bring him back to a calmer state of mind.

The ambiguity of the second line of this verse is important. "What need I strain my heart beyond my ken" may mean "why should he concern himself so much with the fate of people whom he does not know and whose fate is, anyhow, a matter of conjecture?": or "why should he try to see reason in the designs of a Providence to which he can do nothing but submit?" It is the second meaning, I think, which gives the line its particular air of hopelessness and defeat. Hopkins, the philosopher who liked to see reality unravelled, is bewildered and ill at ease. The whole scheme of things is troubling and oppressing him: the "burden and the mystery" are growing intolerable. But his conscious self does not criticise divine Providence; and so in the last two lines he turns his indignation towards the men who deliberately aid the destructive powers which Providence has allowed to surround the human race: who help the devil in his work of spoiling the lovely orderliness of God's creation:

"O but I bear my burning witness though
Against the wild and wanton work of men."

There the poem breaks off: the abruptness and violence of the verse suggest that his feelings have got quite beyond control, so that for the moment poetry is no longer possible.

The implications of this poem have taken us far from Wordsworth and the power of sympathy: I want to return to the comparison with Wordsworth to emphasise one other point: the extremely dramatic quality of Hopkins's work. Here the two poets are opposed. Hopkins thinks in speech to an unusual degree: his poetry is so dependent on words or rather on the art of speech, that it might sometimes be called rhetorical—*That Nature is an Heraclitean Fire* is an example—written, it may be noted, as an offshoot from a sermon. Of Wordsworth, Professor A. A. Jack said that he "taught the language to unform: the art of speech faded away like a thin vapour, and the heart was known." Hopkins's poetry must be read aloud: it fails entirely, as he himself discovered, if it is read by the eye only: and it can well bear to be declaimed, though it does need to be read by the eye as well. Of Wordsworth's poetry I should say myself that it would suffer less than most by being read by the eye only; and it is often peculiarly difficult to read aloud.

Hopkins is, I think, articulate to an unusual degree: Wordsworth very much not so. Hopkins tries to bring even the confused gropings of the mind to the surface, to make them explicit, as in the verse of the *Wreck of the Deutschland* which I have already quoted. He gives expression to little turns and twists of the mind which Wordsworth is content to ignore: a point illustrated by the "o's" and "a's" which are so frequent and often so un-expected in his lyrics.

"And hurls for him, O half hurls earth for him, off
    under his feet."
"Broods with warm breast and with ah! bright
    wings."

Hopkins's fondness for direct speech gives some of his poems the air of being dramatic monologues. The pains which he takes to make himself explicit and articulate sometimes makes his poetry curiously formal and curiously sophisticated. It is as though his personality was divided and one half was taking great pains to make itself clear to the other. I think that, to begin with at any rate, the reader feels himself a spectator rather than a participant in Hopkins's struggles and raptures: it is possible to identify one-self with Wordsworth at once. He catches the reader up and absorbs him; Hopkins keeps him a little aloof, treats him as an audience, does not allow him to take the poet's experiences for his own; the reader shares in them as he might in those of Hamlet or Lear: to some extent he becomes Hamlet or Lear, but still at the same time he knows that he is sitting in the pit or gallery while Lear or Hamlet is walking on the stage.

Here, by the way, it may be worth while to compare Hopkins and Wordsworth in their use of common speech. Wordsworth's habit of using the common speech of common people, in so far as he kept to it, impoverished rather than enriched his vocabulary; there is no need to labour a point already made by Coleridge in *Biographia Literaria*. Hopkins's use of current, not common, idiom is one of his great sources of strength. His modification of English is, so to speak, a sort of Platonic ideal of idiomatic language: "current idiom is, as it were, the presiding spirit in his verse", says Dr Leavis,[1] but it is current idiom made much more compact, more economical, more cryptic: and it is also much more catholic, including more dialects than any English ever spoken. Hopkins's English has the vigour of an early language with the sophistication of a late one; and if he is to be blamed, as Spenser with more cause is blamed, for writing a language never spoken in its entirety at any one time, he might retort, as Spenser might, that it serves his purpose better than any other: and who is to say that that is not an entirely sufficient justification? It is true that Hopkins's use of a self-compiled dialect and his habit of ignoring the conventional rules of syntax contribute to make his poetry appear obscure: I say appear, because I do not think that

[1] *New Bearings in Modern Poetry*, published by Chatto and Windus.

it is really more difficult than that of many poets who have never had the charge of obscurity brought against them.

Hopkins's work from the beginning seems to shew a fondness for dramatic effect. The second version of his poem *St Dorothea*, the Virgin Saint, who after the martyrdom sent flowers from the heavenly garden to convince the scoffer Theophilus, is his earliest dramatic monologue. There is, or was, another version of the poem, in which the lines are divided amongst three speakers, an Angel, the protonotary Theophilus and a Catechumen—a version in which, according to Dr Bridges, the grace and charm of the original is lost. Dr Bridges's strictures are justified. The simplicity of the first version is already a little sophisticated:

> "Lilies I shew you, lilies none,
>   None in Caesar's gardens blow,—
>   And a quince in hand,—not one
>   Is set upon your boughs below:
>   Not set, because their buds not spring;
>   Spring not, 'cause world is wintering."

The saint's childlike pride in her everlasting and unseasonable lilies and her imperishable apple, the childish abbreviation of "because" which is put into her mouth, together with the childish pun on "spring" in the last line build up an effect which in its mixture of innocence and sophistication is something like that produced on the spectator by one of Bernini's child angels, or by the smiling seraph in his sculpture of the piercing of St Teresa's heart in

Santa Maria della Vittoria. In the following verse the effect is continued.

"But these were found in the East and South
Where Winter is the clime forgot.—
The dewdrop on the larkspur's mouth
O should it then be quenchèd not?
In starry water-meads they drew
These drops: which be they? stars or dew?"

The bewilderment which Theophilus expresses as to the nature of the crystal drop on the larkspur, which is presumably part of the saint's celestial bouquet "which be they? stars or dew?" is of a sophisticated kind; it is in fact closely related to the frenzy which, according to Tesauro, in his exposition of the theory of metaphysical poetry, lies behind all metaphor. What is a metaphor but madness, taking one thing for another?

The changes in the later version are in the direction of clearer formulation: the rather precious naïf grace of the earlier poem is gone: but the poem has, so to speak, been tidied up, the scene has been worked out to a logical instead of to an arbitrary conclusion; all its implications have been exposed. The effect produced by the apparition on Theophilus becomes the important part of the poem, and the progress of his mind towards conversion is delineated so clearly and definitely, if a little elliptically, that there is a suggestion that Hopkins is writing for an audience, for people who must be made to understand at once what is going on in the consul's mind. Theophilus goes by clearly marked stages from bewilderment to conviction. Bewilderment—has she gone already? was it a she? was it Dorothea or an angel messenger?—regret at her or its disappearance —realisation that though the apparition has gone it has performed its mission, softening the consul's hard heart to tears. There is a moment in which he reflects on the way in which martyrs make converts, as Dorothea has converted him, and then comes the final impulse to claim the rewards of martyrdom for himself.

> "Proconsul! Is Sapricius near?
> I find another Christian here."

It may be noted incidentally that both versions of Hopkins's poem contain reminiscences of Massinger's Play, *The Virgin Martyr*. The speech with which Theophilus greets the Angel was evidently in Hopkins's mind:

> "What flowers are these?
> In Dioclesian's gardens the most beauteous
> Compared with these, are weeds; is it not February
> The second day she died? frost, ice and snow
> Hang on the beard of winter: where's the sun
> That gilds this summer? pretty sweet boy, say
> In what country shall a man find this garden?"
>
> (Act V. Sc. ii.)

and also this:

> "It is, it is some angel. Vanish'd again!
> Oh, come back, ravishing boy! bright messenger!
> Thou hast, with these mine eyes fixed on thy beauty,
> Illumined all my soul."

Hopkins's poem is, it may be noted, emotionally quite in tune with Massinger's play (excluding of course the comic scenes) both of them taking a wholly sensuous pleasure in the spiritual triumphs of the virgin saint and her attendant angel. Massinger's metrical effects and Massinger's style, like his own, at once colloquial and involved, may very likely have made him a writer who was congenial to Hopkins.

If this were all that could be said about the dramatic character of Hopkins's work, then the dramatic element could not be said to be of much importance. The strain in his work which begins with the *Lines on a Portrait of St Dorothea* is continued and would, if the play had been finished, have reached its climax in *St Winefred's Well*. The printed fragments of the play contain some magnificently rhetorical passages. This, for instance, which is taken from Bruno's speech describing the miraculous virtue of the fountain which sprang up to commemorate Winefred's martyrdom:

"As long as men are mortal and God merciful,
    So long to this sweet spot, this leafy lean-over,
    This Dry Dene, now no longer dry nor dumb, but
        moist and musical
    With the uproll and the downcarol of day and night
        delivering
    Water, which keeps thy name, (for not in róck
        wrítten,
    But in pale water, frail water, wild rash and reeling
        water,
    That will not wear a print, that will not stain a pen,
    Thy venerable record, virgin, is recorded).
    Here to this holy well shall pilgrimages be,

(69)

And not from purple Wales only nor from elmy
    England,
But from beyond seas, Erin, France and Flanders,
    everywhere,
Pilgrims, still pilgrims, móre pílgrims, still more
    poor pilgrims."

But much as Hopkins's poetry as a whole benefits by
his preoccupation with religion, and it does benefit
a great deal, it seems that in dealing with these
stories of miracles he indulges a craving for violent
sensational effects: a craving which vitiates for
instance the *Wreck of the Deutschland*; and there
are signs that it would have vitiated the play. *St
Winefred's Well* as it exists excels only as rhetoric,
or as verse which is, if that is possible, "purely
musical". What emotional substance it has is poor
and crude compared with that of Hopkins's successful poems. An exception might perhaps be made of
the passage in which Caradoc, a character who was
destined by Hopkins to die impenitent after having
murdered the Christian heroine after whom he lusts,
describes the sensation of being a murderer: but
this is a passage which gains nothing from its setting
and which would in fact be more in place in one of
Hopkins's own devotional poems. Such scrupulousness of self-examination, such misery inspired by
guilt is more characteristic perhaps of the very good
than of the very bad.

"I all my being have hacked in half with her neck:
    one part,
  Reason, selfdisposal, choice of better or worse way,

Is corpse now, cannot change; my other self, this
    soul,
Life's quick, this kínd, this kéen self-feeling,
With dreadful distillation of thoughts sour as blood,
Must all day long taste murder."

Hopkins is a dramatic poet, but it is almost safe
to say that he would never have been a playwright,
even if he had kept clear of the dangers which he
courts in *St Winefred's Well*. He demands from his
reader closer attention, and attention maintained
over a longer period than the spectator of a play can
give; his peculiar idiom must, too, have put him at
a disadvantage. But the dramatic monologue is a
form as congenial to him as it was to Browning, and
many of his sonnets might be so described. Hopkins's
uncommon vigour, his impatient desire to make himself perfectly clear (compared with Wordsworth in
this respect he is like a gesticulating excitable Latin,
whose feverish desire to call in every possible aid in
order to make himself perfectly clear is emphasised
by the fact that near him there stands a reserved
and reticent Anglo-Saxon, whose words are few and
whose hands are always in his pockets) combined
with the fact that he is perhaps more than usually
conscious of possessing a body, make it natural to
him to mime. In describing a poem called *Tom's
Garland*, he says that "at the point in the poem in
which the labourer who is described in it leaves off
working" there comes a "violent but effective
hyperbation or suspension, in which the action of
the mind mimics that of the labourer, surveys his

lot, low but free from care: then by a sudden strong act throws it over the shoulder or tosses it away as a light matter". I have already quoted other examples of the way in which in Hopkins's poetry the action of the mind mimics some physical action; it is perhaps in this respect that his work is most dramatic, as it is certainly most original.

Hopkins's poetry does not appeal only to touch and taste and smell, as that of Keats does; it also excites strong muscular responses. There are poems of his—the first octave of *The Windhover* for example, *Tom's Garland*, *Harry Ploughman*, which leave the reader feeling almost as though he had been exercising himself in a gymnasium. *Harry Ploughman* is the poem which illustrates this most clearly.

"Hard as hurdle arms, with a broth of goldish flue
    Breathed round; the rack of ribs; the scooped flank;
        lank
    Rope-over thigh; knee-nave; and barrelled shank—
        Head and foot, shoulder and shank—
    By a grey eye's heed steered well, one crew, fall to;
    Stand at stress. Each limb's barrowy brawn, his thew
    That onewhere curded, onewhere sucked or sank—
        Soared or sank—,
    Though as a beachbole firm, finds his, as at a roll-
        call, rank
    And features, in flesh, what deed he each must do—
        His sinew-service where do."

"He leans to it, Harry bends, look. Back, elbow,
        and liquid waist
    In him, all quail to the wallowing o' the plough—"

The poet is considering Harry with something of the admiration with which a boy expert in mechanical toys looks at an engine. He observes the ploughman limb by limb, feature by feature, until the thrilling moment comes when this marvellous assemblage of parts is put into action, made to "stand at stress". The muscular strength of his whole body is brought into play: the thews of each limb, hard as they are, adapt themselves to the demands made upon them with the alertness and regularity of trained soldiers. The next two lines excite a particularly strong muscular response: the phrase "liquid waist" especially.

Harry Ploughman, like the Windhover and the stormfowl in the Purcell sonnet, is a creature who is intent on exercising all the powers with which he is endowed and who merely as a by-product flashes off beauty, unknown to himself, giving intense pleasure to the eye of the beholder, as well as giving satisfaction to the Creator who sees his creature using its faculties to their utmost. This image is one which seems to give Hopkins at once aesthetic pleasure and spiritual comfort. His own poetry, if he had been able to see it dispassionately, might have pleased him no less than Harry's ploughing and the Windhover's flying; for it evidently engaged all his faculties; it strikes the reader as involving to a peculiar degree all the energies of mind and body.

Wordsworth's poetry is written by a poet living very much out of the body; he is never acutely

conscious of the different parts of his anatomy, as
Hopkins is.

"How a lush-kept, plush-capped sloe
　　Will, mouthed to flesh, burst
　Gush!—flush the man,the being with it,sour or sweet,
　　Brim, in a flash, full."

provokes and records a singularly intense consciousness of the process of drinking a delicious juice, as

"man, the scaffold of score brittle bones"

points to an unusually vivid realisation of the
spillikins-like structure of the skeleton.

"Thou hast bound bones and veins in me, fastened
　　me flesh"

is another line which shews how curiously aware
Hopkins is of the body in which he lives. The eye is
an organ which he is particularly fond of considering
anatomically. In *Elected Silence* he describes the
descent of the two eyelids on the two eyeballs

"Be shellèd, eyes, with double dark."

(There is also a reference here, of course, to the inner
darkness, double dark conveys the idea that the
novice is to preserve not only his eyes but his soul
from impressions of the physical world.) In *Binsey
Poplars* he compares the havoc made by the removal
of the trees to the effect of a single prick on the
eyeball:

"O if we but knew what we do
　　When we delve or hew—
　Hack and rack the growing green!
　　Since country is so tender
　To touch, her being só slender,

(74)

That, like this sleek and seeing ball
But a prick will make no eye at all,
Where we, even where we mean
    To mend her we end her."

While in the first version of the poem on St Dorothea his consciousness of the convex surface of the eyeball makes him compare the reflection which the miracle has left on the retina to the curved rind of a fruit:

"My eyes hold yet the rinds and bright
    Remainder of a miracle."

These examples of Hopkins's consciousness of his body are not drawn from his best poems: there is something a little inharmonious about all of them, in the contexts in which they occur: because it is disagreeable to be made so intensely and exclusively aware of the particular part of the anatomy to which he refers. But on the whole, considering it especially in its less extreme forms, the poet's consciousness of bodily existence and the resulting appeal to physical sensation which is consequently to be found in his poetry are very much to the good. His devotional poems in particular gain by being written, so to speak, with the whole man: he never separates soul and body, never casts off his flesh like a garment in an attempt to emerge all spirit. In describing the most painful kind of spiritual desolation he will use a metaphor which brings in the body:

"I am gall, I am heartburn, God's most deep decree
    Bitter would have me taste: my taste was me."

It was perhaps the same humility which made the Psalmist refer so freely to his bowels and his reins.

Hopkins's insistent remembrance of his physical existence might be taken as a symptom of his peculiar adequacy to experience. For all his unhappiness, spiritual and mental, and judging from his poetry he suffered and was moreover very conscious of suffering a great deal, he never makes any attempt to escape from the discomfort or the danger which confronts him by taking refuge in an imaginary world, nor even in a world purely of the spirit: he never turns to the anodyne of dreams. Religion is sometimes described by those unfriendly to it as a drug: it was certainly not that to Hopkins. It would be difficult too to accuse Hopkins of falling back on his religion instead of using his own inner resources: his poetry affords no means of distinguishing between the two.

Wordsworth, as I have already said, does not give the impression of being conscious in any unusual degree of physical existence; he is interested in the mind's eye rather than in the anatomy of the eyeball: he never praises, never rests in the physical sensation, the sound as it strikes the ear, the sight as it strikes the eye, as Hopkins does. Wordsworth would never have written such a passage as this:

> " When drop-of-blood-and-foam-dapple
>   Bloom lights the orchard-apple
>   And thicket and thorp are merry
>   With silver-surfèd cherry

And azuring-over greybell makes
Wood banks and brakes wash wet like lakes
And magic cuckoo call
Caps, clears, and clinches all"—

a passage which does not go beyond sensuous
apprehension. Wordsworth like his own cuckoo turns
the earth into an unsubstantial faery place: he
communicates to all the sights and sounds that he
describes, the air of things seen and heard in a vision
and by a man who for the time is made all spirit. A
vision not a dream. He does not escape from the
world of sense, but sees it as though it were trans-
figured.

The only poem of Wordsworth that I remember
as shewing him for the time more than usually conscious of existing as a body is the lovely but not
typical *Strange Fits of Passion Have I Known*; and
then it is as a body moving almost in a trance,
hypnotised by the bright moon: the movement of
the horse, the sound of the hooves, the jolting of the
rider in his saddle are all felt with an intensity which
is as considerable as that which characterises
Hopkins's physical sensations; but the intensity of
physical sensation in Wordsworth's poem is part of
the dreamy state which the brightness of the moon
and the rhythmic movements of the horse have
induced in him: he has the sharpened consciousness
of physical existence which sometimes comes just
before sleep: a consciousness by no mean characteristic of him when wide awake.

Wordsworth's peculiar quality as a poet might be

described as a power of etherealising man and his experience; the aim of his poetry is to induce

> "that serene and blessed mood
> In which the affections gently lead us on,—
> Until, the breath of this corporeal frame
> And even the motion of our human blood
> Almost suspended, we are laid asleep
> In body, and become a living soul."

Mr Irving Babbitt, speaking as a humanist and an anti-romantic, sees in such a design the danger of a sham spirituality. An unsympathetic, or a merely unsophisticated reader will often feel that Wordsworth's raptures and Wordsworth's tranquillity are very cheaply bought. He will say, for example, that after hearing how Margaret was forsaken by her husband, waited during nine years for his return and then died in misery, Wordsworth looks at the tall grasses on the wall, sees in them an image of tranquillity and a token that Nature is doing her best to obliterate the traces of human habitation which still mark Margaret's dwelling, and "walks along his road in happiness", quite consoled for Margaret's suffering: he has sympathised with Margaret's distress and the consciousness of doing so has no doubt made him feel very good: but surely the happiness which rewards him is out of all proportion to his exertion. Actually, of course, Wordsworth's joys could not have been obtained without a great deal of self-discipline consistently maintained: he must always have been busy, like Pater's Marius, keeping his mind free of self-preoccupation, and the eyes of his spirit clear. But there is little doubt that Wordsworth does sometimes lay himself open to the charge made by Mr Babbitt and the unfriendly or merely insufficiently sophisticated reader. I suggest that Hopkins's poetry rests on a firmer foundation than Wordsworth's: though I will not say that it has, to continue the metaphor, risen higher. He was certainly exempted from the danger from which Donne in his Litany prays to be delivered:

> "From thinking us all soul, neglecting thus
> Our mutual duties, Lord, deliver us."

Wordsworth, I think, was not; and his poetry is on that account more limited and also so to speak more vulnerable than Hopkins's. Wordsworth is praised by Matthew Arnold for having dealt with "joy in widest commonalty spread", pleasure available to everyone. But though the joy communicated by Wordsworth's poetry is available to everyone it is available to them only in certain circumstances and above all in certain moods. The way of living and facing life suggested by Hopkins's poetry seems likely to be satisfactory under more different sets of conditions than Wordsworth's way of life could meet. I do not mean merely that Hopkins had a better philosophy, that an enlightened Catholicism has the advantage over a sentimental Pantheism: I mean that Hopkins's "mould of mind" (itself in turn moulded by his philosophy, but one must not stop there) was one which produced poems which are, to change the metaphor, hardier plants, more able to support all weathers and serviceable for more purposes than Wordsworth's.

VI

Anxious to forestall the criticisms with which he thought his friend's work certain to be confronted, Dr Bridges in the edition of Hopkins's work which he published in 1918 thought it advisable to admit beforehand that Hopkins's poetry was odd, the product of a mind which was extreme in all things, and that there was much in it which was bound to offend those who were solicitous, as he himself was, to maintain a continuous literary decorum; that it was in fact obscure.

When Dr Bridges calls Hopkins's poetry odd he is evidently using the word as a term of blame: but a critic who does not share Bridges's solicitude for a continuous literary decorum can admit that Hopkins's poetry is odd without thinking any less of it on that account. The oddness of which Dr Bridges accuses it is of a kind which can be modified by time; now that Hopkins has influenced so many other poets he does not stand quite alone as he did in 1918: his poetry is less unusual, less isolated. The charge of oddness, as the word is used by Dr Bridges, is not a very serious one, except to people holding the same opinions. But Hopkins himself feared that his poetry might lapse into what must be judged as oddness by his own standards: and that is a more serious matter. "As air, melody, is what strikes me most of all in music, and design in painting, so design, pattern, or what I am in the habit of calling *inscape*, is what I above all aim at in poetry. Now it is the virtue of design, pattern or inscape to be distinctive, and it is the vice of distinctiveness to become queer. This vice I cannot have escaped", he wrote in 1879. The oddness of Hopkins, then, is connected with his theory of "inscape", a word which he coined himself to describe the pattern which makes every fragment of creation, every "bead of being", to use his own phrase, individual and unique. "Spanish chestnuts: their inscape bold, jutty, somewhat oak-like." "Looking at the elms from underneath you saw every wave in every twig—and to the hangers and flying sprays it restored, to the eye, the inscapes they had lost." "I saw a brindled heaven, the moon just masked by a blue spot pushing its way through the darker cloud, underneath, and, on the skirts of the rack, bold, long, flakes whitened and swaled like feathers, below the garden with the heads of the trees and shrubs furry grey: I read a broad careless inscape flowing throughout." "Outscape" occurs once in the extracts from his juvenile prose given by Fr. Lahey.

"We passed through a country of pale grey rocky hills of a strong and simple outscape covered with fields of waving green vines." Here evidently it describes the shape which the hills take in relation to their background.

Closely allied to his conception of inscape is his conception of what he calls the "sake". "I mean by it the being a thing has outside itself, as a voice by its echo, a face by its reflection, a body by its shadow, a man by his name, fame, or memory, *and also* that in the thing by virtue of which especially it has this being abroad, and that is something distinctive, marked, specifically or individually speaking: as for a voice and echo, clearness: for a reflected image, light, brightness: for a shadow-casting body, bulk: for a man genius, great achievements, amiability and so on." The difference between sake and inscape is partly that inscape is there whether seen or not: inscape is the result of the object's relation to its creator. "Instress", another of his coinages, describes the particular effect which a thing may have upon a particular person. He speaks, for example, of feeling a "charm and instress of Wales" meaning both that he was conscious of the atmosphere of Wales as distinct from all others and that this atmosphere was charged with a special significance for himself. Instress is used at times as though to describe inscape as it is apprehended by senses other than the eye.

Fr. Lahey gives examples of Hopkins's use of these words occurring in his prose diary. Of these "All the world is full of inscape, and chance left free to act falls into an order as well as purpose" is the most significant; inscape in plants and trees and skies proves that beauty, and orderly beauty at that, can come into being almost at random, or in a way baffling to man, and therefore known only to God.

Hopkins's word-coinings all indicate that unusually strong preoccupation with individuality of which something has already been said. It was presumably his love of the individual which made Duns Scotus "him of all men who most" swayed Hopkins's "spirit to peace". His love of and value for the individual seems to have preceded his discovery of Scotism. The latter became a passion with him presumably because it fitted in so well with his own beliefs and feelings. In the Isle of Man during his novitiate he began "to get hold of the copy of Scotus on the Sentences in the Bodley Library and was flush with a new stroke of enthusiasm. It may come to nothing or it may be a mercy from God. But just then when I took in any inscape of the sky or sea I thought of Scotus". From such an account of Duns Scotus's philosophy as M. Étienne Gilson's it is clear enough that it must have been congenial to Hopkins.

"While for St Thomas it is matter which gives its individuality to form, Duns Scotus places the principle of individuation inside form itself. The reason why Peter is not merely a man, but a particular man called Peter is that the human form and by consequence Peter's very essence already bears the mark of particularity, so that the essence of the individual contains a principle of contraction and limitation which restricts its universality."

"Evidently in Scotism individuality has a much greater degree of reality than in Thomism. It is no

(83)   6-2

longer added to form as an exterior accident, material and accidental: on the contrary, it is individuality which confers upon the existing being its final perfection, so to speak its final maturity.... His anxiety to safeguard as completely as possible the originality of the individual is equally evident in Duns Scotus's conception of the priority of the will and in his doctrine of liberty.... The will alone is the total cause of the volition in the will: nihil aliud a voluntate est causa totalis volitionis in voluntate.... St Thomas has the genius for rational order and was perhaps the greatest arranger of ideas that humanity has ever known. Duns Scotus is rather an inventor than an arranger. It might be said that with him and his philosophy the Christian conception of a God who is infinite and a Creator comes for the first time to full consciousness of itself. In delivering the Infinite Being from every kind of determination, even from that of archetypes conceived by the act of an essence which can only conceive itself, Duns Scotus asserts the rights of the Christian God, and defends them instinctively against the contamination of Greek thought."[1]

Hopkins seems from his own account to have been one of the three Scotists to be found in England: and this in spite of the fact that, as Fr. Lahey says, Jesuit theologians are Thomists. The very orderliness and completeness which its supporters claim as the great merits of St Thomas's system are likely to have been in a way repugnant to Hopkins. St Thomas's system was deliberately and painstakingly constructed: Scotus's, fragmentary as it is, seems to

[1] *La Philosophie au Moyen Âge*, par Étienne Gilson, pp. 239–242, Collection Payot.

have grown. Order, to be congenial to Hopkins, must be organic, not superimposed.

It is clear from what has been said here and in the earlier part of this essay that Hopkins had an extraordinary solicitude for individuality and that he must to some extent have cultivated an awareness of his difference from, rather than his likeness to, the rest of human beings. He is always solicitous to

"Deal out that being indoors each one dwells":

his poetry is the result of an attempt to expose the inscape of his own personality. It must be remembered, however, that by Hopkins's theory this inscape, this existence-pattern, as Aldous Huxley calls it, is clearest not when the man is abandoning himself in a Rousseau-ish way to his expansive instincts but when he is exerting his faculties to the utmost, in an effort at once disciplined and spontaneous: it is when he is "strung by duty" that he is "strained to beauty", the beauty that accompanies the revelation of the pattern of his being.

As Hopkins himself says, so much care for the distinctive, the individual must at times make his work odd, in the sense in which he himself would have admitted it to be a term of blame. His extreme originality is in itself a merit: but as a result of it he had no touchstone by which to try his utterances: he was compelled to rely on his own judgment in a degree almost unparalleled. That his dialect and his prosody were, as he himself said, "the spontaneous expression of his poetical feelings" is beyond a doubt: but in default of any norm, any exterior standard by which he might judge his poetry, his expression of individuality did at times, though far less often than any critic warned of his experiments would have anticipated, run amuck. Long before the end of his life he had reached a certainty about his own standards which gave his poetry the air of inevitability which Goethe speaks of as an attribute of all great verse: he had done what some critics say is impossible to one man, he had not only created a form but brought it to perfection. But I should be loth to say that there is nothing odd in the *Wreck of the Deutschland*. Poetry which aims at being an exposition of inscape, at laying bare the pattern of the poet's *bead of being*, can only be successful when that inscape is fully developed: it depends to an unusual degree on the maturity and on the self-consciousness of the artist. In the *Wreck of the Deutschland* Hopkins is not sure enough of himself, not certain enough that the traits which he is expressing are those of his own individuality and not foreign to him, not to impress the reader with a sense that the poet is deviating into oddity—oddity which would have been judged as oddity by his own mature standards. If Hopkins's poetry had not had the whole force of his personality behind it, it would have become odd and frigid in the extreme. On the rare occasions in which in his poetry he allows his fancy to run wild the reader sees very clearly how great a feat he is accomplishing ordinarily in maintaining the right balance. If Hopkins had written often as a mere virtuoso, merely intoxicated with his skill and ingenuity, his verse would have been intolerable; more so than the occasional virtuosities of so chastened a poet as, say, his friend Bridges: it was the price which Hopkins had to pay for being a disciple of no school but his own.

Odd in the sense of being the product of a mind which deflects from the normal in a way not to be desired Hopkins's poetry considered as a whole is not. Nor is it odd in the sense of standing apart in essentials from what is often called the mainstream of English poetry. Hopkins's successful poems, and those that are not are very few, appeal to no freakish or abnormal mood in the reader. They bear very strongly the marks of their author's idiosyncrasies but the idiosyncrasies are those of a mind singularly well-poised and for all its extreme sensitiveness singularly healthy.

Hopkins's "obscurity" is in less need of defence to-day than it was during his lifetime when it was felt by himself and by his friend Bridges to make publication impracticable. Dixon, Patmore and Bridges, the three friends, all poets, who seem to have been the only people who during his lifetime saw much of his work, seem all to have been baffled by its obscurity. Patmore admitted himself slow in appreciating art. "My difficulty in getting at anything very new is, as I have said before, greater than that of most persons; and sometimes that difficulty seems insuperable", he writes after reading some of Hopkins's manuscripts. Dr Bridges, as an upholder of what may roughly be called the classic tradition, was likely to put a high value on ease and lucidity as ends in themselves: and that being so he was bound at times to fail in responding to Hopkins's poems, though his response to them was much more nearly adequate than Patmore's. Dixon's, to judge from the scanty evidence available at the moment, seems to have been a mind more congenial to Hopkins's than that of either of the others. It was Dixon who found the excellent phrase "terrible pathos" to describe the peculiar quality of Hopkins's work; and in his own poetry there is much that must have appealed and indeed did appeal to Hopkins, as we know from Bridges's preface to Dixon's poems. The Pre-Raphaelite richness of Dixon's work was one of the qualities which Hopkins most admired. "The extreme delight I felt when I read the line 'her eyes like lilies shaken by the trees' was more than any single line in poetry ever gave me", he writes in a letter generously describing the pleasure given him by Dixon's poetry. Dixon's poetry has, too, a Wordsworthian strain which must have interested Hopkins. Dixon is much occupied with what he calls "the unanswered question which asks the meaning of natural phenomena considered as data from which man's mind may deduce or conjecture his relation to the mind of the Universe...the unanswerable question defies logic and any plain statement of it quickly takes it out of poetry". Dixon's way of solving the problem seems to have been to give up inquiring into Nature's significance and simply to submit to her good influences: a passivity quite foreign to Hopkins who either busies himself with constructing parallels between God's workings in nature and his workings in the sphere of divine revelation, or else, with a fling of the heart, an impulsive, instinctive movement of the whole being, breaks through and almost rejects natural phenomena,

"hurls for him, O half hurls earth for him off under
    his feet."

The two poets have in common, however, a peculiar devotion to the wild aspects of nature, which, because they are peculiarly baffling to human logic, seem to them to be particularly characteristic of the workings of the divine mind. *Wayward Water* is the title of one of Dixon's most charming and characteristic nature poems.

> "Sky that rollest ever
>   It is given to thee
> To roll above the river
>   Rolling to the sea.
>
> Truer is thy mirror
>   In the lake or sea;
> But thou lovest error
>   More than constancy.
>
> And the river running
>   Fast into the sea,
> His wild hurry shunning
>   All thy love and thee,

Not a moment staying
To return thy smiles
Sees thee still displaying
All thy sunny wiles:

Till thou fallest weeping;
Then more furiously
All his wild waves leaping
Rush into the sea."

There is the same love of wildness in the one poem
of Dixon's usually found in anthologies, the poem
which begins:

"The feathers of the willow
Are half of them grown yellow
  Above the swelling stream;
And ragged are the bushes,
And rusty now the rushes
  And wild the clouded gleam."

Hopkins's *Inversnaid* shews the same joy in the wild
untidy freshness which may be found in the most
faded and monotonous scenes.

The letter which Hopkins sent to Dixon in 1878
suggested that the two poets had also a common
grief. When Hopkins says that he makes bold to
write to Dixon, though almost a stranger to him,
because "I knew what I should feel myself in your
position if I had written and published works, the
extreme beauty of which the author himself most
keenly feels, and they had fallen out of sight at once
and have been (you will not mind my saying it, as
it is, I suppose, plainly true) almost wholly unknown": when he says that he feels it "a sort of

duty of charity to make up, so far as one voice can do, for the disappointment you must, as least at times, I think, have felt over your rich and exquisite work almost thrown away", he seems to the reader to be describing a situation which is in fact his own, except that Hopkins had not published his work. The isolation and frustration of which Dixon must have been conscious were present to a still greater degree in Hopkins's own poetic life. It is not surprising that he should at times have lacked the "rapture" of an "inspiration" when one considers that he had almost no external stimulus to creative work.

Without a closer knowledge of the relationship between Hopkins and Dixon than may be had at the moment, it is impossible to say whether Dixon complained of the obscurity of Hopkins's work as much as Bridges did. The notes to the Poems record that Dixon was as much baffled as Bridges was by that uncomfortable *tour-de-force*, *Tom's Garland*; but since that is possibly the oddest of all Hopkins's poems, Dixon cannot on that score alone be dismissed as an unsympathetic reader who stood unwearyingly to the defence of a "continuous literary decorum".

However, Dr Bridges at the time, and a number of readers since, who cannot on that score be dismissed as unintelligent, have found Hopkins's poetry obscure: and the charge must be considered. It may be noted that not all the readers who find his poetry obscure dislike it on that account. Mr Aldous Huxley, for instance, in one of his essays in the collection called *Music at Night*,[1] says: "Solving riddles is an occupation that appeals to almost all of us. All poetry consists of riddles, to which the answers are occasionally, as in Dante's case, scientific or metaphysic. One of the pleasures we derive from poetry is precisely the cross-word puzzler's delight in working out a problem. For certain people this pleasure is peculiarly intense. Nature's puzzle solvers, they tend to value poetry in proportion as it is obscure. I have known such people who, too highbrow to indulge in the arduous imbecilities of cross-word and acrostic, sought satisfaction for an imperious yearning in the sonnets of Mallarmé and the more eccentric verses of Gerard Hopkins". One suspects that the poet would have been just as happy not to receive the approval of such readers as Mr Huxley describes, if there are any. It is a good thing that the reading of poetry should be considered as a process in which the reader plays an active not a passive part: but to reduce the pleasure given by poetry to that given by cross-word puzzle is to leave poetry with very little excuse for its existence: the pains taken by the poet being so much out of proportion to the pleasure given to the reader. Ben Jonson, in these matters possibly a profounder critic, remarked that: "Whatsoever loseth the grace and clearness converts into a riddle; the obscurity is marked, but not the value"; he was of the opinion that the pleasure of solving a riddle was very inferior

---

[1] Published by Chatto and Windus.

to that which poetry ought to give: and if Jonson had condemned Hopkins for "losing the grace and clearness" and turning his poetry into a riddle, Hopkins would, I think, have found it a serious accusation: though it is true that as a "classical" critic who held that "Custom is the most certain mistress of language, as the public stamp makes the current money", Jonson begins with assumptions inimical to a just appreciation of Hopkins. Unless the reader is prepared to accept as legitimate any poetic device which the poet cares to use, provided that he uses it successfully, Hopkins's poetry will cause him nothing but discomfort: but it is difficult to find any good reason for not making that concession.

A good deal of the obscurity of which Hopkins has been accused must have proceeded from the attitude of the reader. Wordsworth says somewhere that the poet himself has to create the taste by which he is to be enjoyed: a remark which does not apply to all poets, not even to all great and original poets, but which is quite true of Hopkins. Hopkins had no opportunity of winning a public gradually, nor had he, as some poets have had, any minor predecessor to put the reader into the attitude required. Many of the complaints of his obscurity are nothing more than symptoms of the public's difficulty in cultivating the taste by which he is to be enjoyed: pains of adjustment. After all, Wordsworth, who is now spoken of habitually as the most limpid of poets, was accused of obscurity while the public was in the process of adjusting itself to his own peculiar kind of poetry: and so was the young Tennyson.

Admittedly Hopkins's poetry presents more impediments to hurried and superficial reading than Wordsworth's does: it takes longer to disentangle the prose meaning of the *Wreck of the Deutschland* than it does to arrive at a satisfactory paraphrase of, say, *Lucy Gray*: though I am not certain that it takes longer to arrive at full enjoyment. An extraordinary number of readers seem still to believe that the essential joy of reading poetry is in the disentanglement of the logical thread: and that if this takes a long while the poet is to be blamed for obscurity. If this is really so, one wonders why they do not prefer to read short synopses of poems, instead of the poems themselves. As Mr Richards has said, Hopkins deliberately makes it impossible for the reader to hurry over his lines, and he demands to be read slowly, and with the ear, so that the full content of his poetry may have time to appear. The unusual richness and complexity of his verse makes this demand not only justifiable, but necessary. In any case the demand is not a new one. A man who read the famous speeches in *Troilus and Cressida* in the hope of disentangling the logical thread at a glance would be likely, in Johnson's phrase, to hang himself.

M. Valéry says of one difficult author: "Ses ouvrages ne sont pas d'une lecture bien aisée. Mais je ne cesse de répondre qu'il faut bénir les auteurs difficiles de notre temps". I take it that M. Valéry is not grateful to difficult authors because they give the reader an activity which may take the place of solving cross-word puzzles, an activity which only involves one faculty of the mind, but, on the contrary, because they demand from the reader that effort of the whole being which is necessary to the appreciation of most great poetry, but which the educated public as a whole seems less and less willing to give. In demanding this effort Hopkins is surely anything but exorbitant.

Hopkins may also be found obscure by readers who still hold to the belief that poetry should be unambiguous in its logical meaning, though it is pretty certain that much poetry obtains its effects by ambiguity of some kind. Tennyson, a sufficiently lucid poet, when asked whether he meant this or that by a certain phrase in one of his poems admitted that he meant both, and Mr Empson in his *Seven Types of Ambiguity* has argued that ambiguity is the backbone of most good poems. Again, experiments shew that even very scrupulous and careful readers differ in their interpretation of the logical content of so apparently straightforward a poem as Wordsworth's sonnet, *Sole listener, Duddon!*[1] If the great poets have meant their meaning to be unambiguous they have failed miserably. Hopkins's poetry is, as it happens, less ambiguous than most in respect of mere logical meaning: the ambiguity is usually in the implications of mood and attitude in the poet, as

[1] *See* I. A. Richards, *Principles of Literary Criticism*, published by Kegan Paul.

in *The Windhover*, where he writes in a mood in which he is at once consoled and despairing: he feels both attitudes as possibilities and seems to adopt neither to the exclusion of the other.

Patmore was amused at Hopkins's claiming for himself "the extreme of popular style"[1]: and perhaps, taking into account the strangeness of his vocabulary and the involutions of his syntax, the claim does appear a little outrageous. But it is easy enough to see what Hopkins meant: in my own experience ingenuous readers with a taste for poetry not modified by current academic standards do usually admit that Hopkins's poetry pleases at once, long before it is thoroughly understood: it gives pleasure at once by its sound and by its bold and rich suggestiveness as the gorgeous speeches in Shakespeare do. This power of pleasing or at any rate rousing interest instantaneously must be held to characterise the popular poet. Hopkins's poetry has bold effects and subtle effects: if the latter cannot be appreciated except after many readings the former make their market at once. Hopkins might have hoped to please, as Shakespeare does, on several different levels.

Hopkins's poetry makes it more difficult than usual for the reader to delude himself into thinking that a single reading will take him as far as he needs to go. But the standards by which a poet who requires to be read slowly is judged guilty of some offence at once social and aesthetic cannot be main-

[1] See Lahey, p. 61.

tained in seriousness to-day. When the Duchesse de Guermantes told Proust's hero to see a certain masterpiece if only from the top of a 'bus he reflected that the implication of her remark was that the eye is a sort of camera " qui prend des instantanés ". It is not: but more people than Proust's Duchess assume that it is.

Like as he is in some way to the poets of our own generation, Hopkins does not come under the condemnation launched at the moderns by Mr Max Eastman: he does not write "private" poetry. "If all literature may be described as a verbal communication of values, the modernists may be described as absorbed in the values to the neglect of the act of communicating them. They are unsociable poets, unfriendly, and in extreme cases their language approaches that of the insane or idiotic. Indeed the word 'idiot' means in its origin nothing more slanderous of the character of much of their writing than 'private'." Hopkins is not a poet whose poems are intended to be poems in Mr Eastman's phrase "between me and myself". He does not limit the circle of his readers, as Eliot is said to do to some extent, by fondness for allusions: nor does he use private symbols as Auden does. For instance, a passage from the diary shews that the bluebell was to Hopkins a symbol of the beauty of Christ. "I do not think I have ever seen anything more beautiful than the bluebell I have been looking at. I know the beauty of our Lord by it. Its inscape is mixed of strength and grace." But the bluebell never occurs in his poems as a private symbol: he does not assume that it has for others the significance which it has for him. In this sense again he might be called a popular poet.

It is a question whether or not a poet sets limits to the public to which he can appeal by writing poetry which cannot be appreciated unless the reader adopts at any rate temporarily certain religious beliefs. The bulk of Hopkins's poetry depends on the dogmas of Christianity or describes experience of a kind which is generally supposed to be familiar only to Christians. But the beliefs are not of an esoteric nature: the religious attitude is one with which we are all at any rate traditionally familiar: and although such a poem as the sonnet *Patience*, for instance, will no doubt please a Christian reader who likes it more than it will please a non-Christian reader who likes it, the increase of pleasure which it gives to the reader who, from his own experience, is already familiar with the state of mind which Hopkins dealt with, comes from considerations which are not strictly relevant to the poem itself.

In spite of his strong religious preoccupations Hopkins seems never to have deceived himself into thinking, as Wordsworth did, and as Tennyson seems to have done as a result of the force of public opinion, that the moral or dogmatic content of his poetry was what was most important in it. Perhaps the poet who is also to some extent the inventor of a creed is more apt to lay stress on the importance of the "ideas" in his poetry than the poet whose creed has been discovered and shaped for him beforehand.

Hopkins takes his Catholicism for granted: it has become part of him, as perhaps the pantheism of Wordsworth and Tennyson's creed, in which honest doubt fought with a perhaps dishonest optimism, never became part of their respective protagonists: Hopkins's soundness on this point is a rarer merit than might be supposed. There seems, for example, to have been a time when Mr Yeats thought that the doctrines—Rosicrucian and so on—which he expounded in his poetry gave them all their value. It is not only the Christian poet who is exposed to the danger of thinking of his poetry merely as being a vehicle for his ideas.

It has been said and I think truly, that Hopkins is not a poet whose poetry springs directly from his religious vocation, as, for instance, Herbert's does. Herbert speaks of his poetry as being

> "that which while I use
> I am with Thee",

and his poems often strike the reader as being not merely descriptions of religious experience but the means of religious experience. This is not true of Hopkins's poetry, with the exception perhaps of *The Windhover*. Very few of Hopkins's poems deal immediately with his intercourse with Christ. *The Windhover*, and the sonnet *Thou art indeed just, Lord*, are the only poems in which he directly addresses Christ; and perhaps in *The Windhover* he is speaking at, rather than to, our Lord: he is not so much addressing him as allowing him to overhear his complaint. In most of the religious sonnets Hopkins is talking to himself and deriving a sort of phantom consolation from the act of rehearsing the painful events, or the painfulness of the lack of event, in his spiritual life. Herbert seems to have an interlocutor always at hand: he addresses Christ directly, certain that he is there: Hopkins says that his cries are like dead letters sent

"'to dearest him that lives, alas, away'",

and in the absence of the person to whom he would wish to talk he is driven to be himself both speaker and listener:

"What sights we, heart, saw, ways we went."

My own feeling is that if there were happy moments in Hopkins's spiritual life, moments when he was conscious of the longed-for presence, he would still not have chosen to celebrate these in his poems: poetry was to him a solace in grief, not a means of prolonging joy. In moments of complete spiritual happiness he would have had no need to write poems; the poem was to him a means of resolving a conflict, of establishing an equilibrium and in happiness he would have reached the balance and the peace already. If he ever achieves tranquillity in his poetry it is only as a result of stating with unusual candour the conflict which occupies him; it is the tranquillity which comes as a result of a deliberate suspension of anxiety: seeing all the possibilities of distress he yet holds himself back and will follow none of the ways of worrying suggested to him by his reason. The only tranquillity which he knows is the tranquillity which comes of knowing that you have missed no opportunity of taking stock of your situation; that whatever else may happen to you you will not be taken aback nor deceived. There is a kind of phantom happiness to be found in admitting oneself unhappy: this Hopkins seems sometimes to have enjoyed.

For convenience sake Hopkins's religious poetry may be divided into two classes, though it is not always possible to distinguish clearly between them. In one I shall put poems which are capable of being used as aids to devotion because they offer illustrations of the truths of Christian dogma and of the working of God's providence—poems in which there might be said to be some didactic intention, however slight: in the other the poems which deal with Hopkins's experience as an individual soul rather than as one of the many members of the Christian Church. The distinction is sometimes stated as that between dogmatic poetry and devotional poetry. It may be noted here that Mr Herbert Read in an article in *New Verse* classifies the poems which I should call poems of devotion as poems of doubt. It seems to me that Mr Read fails to make the distinction between disbelieving one's religion and being unhappy in it: he writes as though religion meant no more than giving one's assent to a set of formulae: and so whenever Hopkins is unhappy he is assumed by Mr Read to be regretting the fact that he had ever made the fatal motion of complying with the doctrines of the Church. But Hopkins's religion at any rate must be considered as involving also a personal relationship with Christ; and even if it were allowable to deduce from the signs of unhappiness in his poems that he regretted having entered upon this relationship (a deduction which seems by no means justified) that would not be the same thing as saying that he doubted the existence of the person.

On the other hand it is, I think, true that most of the little devotional poetry which has been written in the last few generations stresses the pains rather than the joys of religious experience. Hopkins and the T. S. Eliot of *Ash Wednesday* sometimes write in the same tone of wistful self-pity: rather as though they were regretting the natural life and the natural scale of values: they seem to acknowledge that if their spirit is broken it is for their own good and yet they cannot help wishing that it were not so. "If God tires you, tell him that he tires you", says one writer on the spiritual life. Hopkins and Eliot often practise this sad frankness. Candour and sadness are audible in the very rhythms of *Ash Wednesday*.[1]

"Wavering between the profit and the loss
  In this brief transit where the dreams cross
  The dream crossed twilight between birth and dying
  (Bless me, father) though I do not wish to wish
      these things
  From the wide window towards the granite shore
  The white sails still fly seaward, seaward flying
  Unbroken wings

[1] Published by Faber and Faber.

And the lost heart stiffens and rejoices
In the lost lilac and the lost sea-voices
And the weak spirit quickens to rebel
For the bent golden-rod and the lost sea smell
Quickens to recover
The cry of quail and the whirling plover
And the blind eye creates
The empty forms between the ivory gates
And smell renews the salt savour of the sandy
    earth."

There is candour—the writer is taking great pains to represent justly his own spiritual condition—he will not pretend to joys that he does not know—sadness, undoubtedly: represented as a longing for the unspoilt spontaneous natural life, for which the strenuous spiritual life cannot be a satisfactory substitute: Eliot's "whirling plover" is a symbol reminiscent of Hopkins's kestrel. There is also in Eliot's devotional poetry, and in most of Hopkins's an air of intense fatigue.

"May the judgment not be too heavy upon us
Because these wings are no longer wings to fly
But only fans to beat the air
The air that is now thoroughly small and dry
Smaller and dryer than the will
Teach us to care and not to care
Teach us to sit still."

The typical figure is Simeon who is too tired to want to adapt himself to the new dispensation, glad as he is to welcome it.

"Let thy servant depart
Having seen thy salvation."

The ungracious candour of Eliot's Magi may also be noted:

> "A cold coming we had of it
> Just the worst time of the year
> For a journey and such a long journey:
> The ways deep and the weather sharp
> The very dead of winter."

Earlier writers might have thought it almost impious to represent the Three Kings as emphasising the physical discomforts of their journey to this extent. The discomfort which these discoverers of Christ experience is not merely physical either: the revelation of God as a child is repugnant to their ordinary ways of feeling and thinking and though they have no choice but to believe they will not pretend to be happy in their belief.

> "All this was a long time ago, I remember,
> And I would do it again, but set down
> This set down
> This: were we led all that way for
> Birth or Death? There was a Birth, certainly
> We had evidence and no doubt. I had seen birth
>   and death
> But had thought they were different: this Birth was
> Hard and bitter agony for us, like Death, our death.
> We returned to our places, these Kingdoms,
> But no longer at ease here, in the old dispensation,
> With an alien people clutching their gods.
> I should be glad of another death."

This is a poem which suggests that the writer is living in a world which for a Christian is very much out of joint. His position is sadder than that of his predecessors in that he cannot exult over the pagans, as they did, secure in the fact that

> "Solid joys and lasting treasures
> Only Sion's children know",

because he is above all conscious of the pains of religion here and now. It is not giving him delight nor emotional satisfaction: he is reduced to clinging to it only by the will. The condition is one of which I believe spiritual experts often approve, as giving scope for the exercise of disinterested love of God and the exercise of fortitude and patience: but if it lasts as with Hopkins it seems to have done it must make a sad life. The poetry of Hopkins and Eliot suggests that in this "setting part of time" Christian poets are suffering from a sort of spiritual old age: but it may of course be only that both poets are, for different reasons, very tired.

The poem of Hopkins's which most resembles Eliot's is the sonnet of which the motto is "Justus quidem tu es, Domine, si disputem tecum: verumtamen justa loquar ad te: Quare via impiorum prosperatur", etc. In this poem he is much appalled by the agony, the thwarting of his good desires, the fatigue which his religion seems to bring on him: he complains as candidly and directly as Eliot's Magi: he presents his case fully and scrupulously, so that although the poem leaves an impression of great spiritual fatigue, it also creates an impression of extreme intellectual vigour: and this is characteristic. Hopkins may be spiritually and emotionally tired, but he is never languid, he never acquiesces in his fatigue, as for instance Arnold might. He reminds himself constantly that he "can something hope, wish day come, not choose not to be."

The majority of readers, of English readers at any rate, are apt to distrust poetry dealing with intimate religious experience. Is the poet deceiving himself— do such things actually happen? they ask. If these happen, ought they to be talked about? The American editor of Herbert's poems says that his religious love lyrics will seem to some half-sinful, presumably because they deal with matter which ought not to be discussed. Many people think there is no such thing as mystical experience, and some people who have no doubt of its reality will be prepared to disapprove of the poet who has made of it a subject for poetry.

"Poetical devotion", says Dr Johnson,[1] "cannot often please.... The doctrines of religion may, indeed, be defended in a didactic poem, and he who has the happy power of arguing in verse, will not lose it because his subject is sacred. A poet may describe the beauty and the grandeur of Nature, the flowers of the Spring, and the harvests of Autumn, the vicissitudes of the tide and the revolutions of the sky, and praise the Maker for his works, in lines which no reader can lay aside. The subject of the disputation is not piety, but the motives to piety: that of the description is not God, but the works of God.

"But contemplative piety, or the intercourse between God and the human soul, cannot be poetical.

[1] *Life of Waller.*

(106)

Man, admitted to implore the mercy of his Creator, and plead the merits of his Redeemer, is already in a higher state than poetry can confer.

"The essence of poetry is invention: such invention, as by producing something unexpected, surprises and delights. The topics of devotion are few, and being few are universally known; but few as they are, they can be made no more: they can receive no grace from novelty of sentiment and very little from novelty of expression."

I should imagine that, as a rule, those who know what contemplative piety is would feel that they were in a higher state than poetry could confer: but evidently there are exceptions. The existence of two such poets as Hopkins and Herbert proves that poetry and contemplative piety can be reconciled: though it is perhaps true that the kind of person usually described as a saint would lose all sense of poetic values in his sense of the religious. The balance can be struck only by a person who still hovers between the two worlds, the spiritual and the natural. Johnson's second objection is also sound: the inventive powers of the poet who writes of such topics as these is necessarily hampered. He has to maintain religious as well as poetic integrity: he cannot invent situations which are not actual, he must not pretend to degrees of goodness which he has not reached. In Cowper's words:

"The Christian, in whose soul, though now distress'd
Lives the dear thought of joys he once possessed
When all his glowing language issued forth
With God's deep stamp upon its current worth,

Will speak without disguise, and must impart,
Sad as it is, his undissembling heart,
Abhors constraint, and dares not feign a zeal,
Or seem to boast a fire he does not feel."

But Johnson's objections mean only that "contemplative piety" (it should be noted that Johnson is not using "contemplative" in the sense in which it is used by writers on mysticism) will not often produce good poetry, not that it never will. The poetry which it does produce is likely to be all the more valued because of its rarity.

Of the poems in which Hopkins is exciting himself or his reader to a fuller realisation of the truths of his religion, the longest, if not the most important is the *Wreck of the Deutschland*, of which Dr Bridges says that it stands logically as well as chronologically, in the front of Hopkins's book, "like a great dragon folded in the gate to forbid all entrance and confident in his strength from past success". For seven years after his entry into the Jesuit Order Hopkins wrote nothing, and it was with the *Wreck of the Deutschland* that he broke silence. It is a poem of thirty-five stanzas, very elaborate in its structure, and almost all Hopkins's subsequent poetry may be said to be in germ here, all, that is, except the "terrible sonnets" which I think are in a class apart. The obscurity of the *Wreck of the Deutschland* has on the whole been exaggerated: but it is true that it is not a complete success: there is something in it which strikes one as artificial in the bad sense. I think it is that in places at any rate the poet has tried to make himself believe that his feelings on the subject under consideration were more intense than was actually the case, at any rate at the moment of writing. The poem savours too much of St Ignatius's method of meditation, in which the will excites the emotions: here one feels that the will is forcing the emotions and forcing them too roughly. The poem moves at a tremendous speed, but with all its rushing the poet does not succeed in allowing himself to be carried away.

The theme of the shipwreck occurs twice in Hopkins's poetry. Besides the *Wreck of the Deutschland* there is the *Loss of the Eurydice* which has the faults of the former—notably a perfervidness which often strikes the reader as uncomfortably forced—without its merits. Hopkins found that the wreck of the boat carrying among its many passengers five Franciscan nuns who had just been exiled from Germany touched him very closely: the event seems to have been intimately associated with a crisis in his own spiritual history. Again, the shipwreck is for him a spectacular and peculiarly notable instance of God's dealings with man, of the way in which he shows himself in foul weather as well as in fair. The "bay of his blessing", says Hopkins, using an architectural metaphor, "has a dark side", and this is the fact which the poem illustrates. The naïf and primitive element in Hopkins's mind is attracted by the manifestation of God in his aspect of terror.

> "Be adored among men
> God, three-numberèd form;

> Wring thy rebel, dogged in den,
> Man's malice, with wrecking and storm.
> Beyond saying sweet, past telling of tongue,
> Thou art lightning and love, I found it, a winter and
>   warm;
> Father and fondler of heart thou hast wrung
> Hast thy dark descending and most art merciful
>   then."

"Thou art lightning and love, *I found it*", he says.

The *stress*, to use his own word, which Hopkins feels when he thinks of the shipwreck occurs because the shipwreck illustrates on a grander scale the truth which his own experience at the moment is teaching him: namely, that God's dealings with men have a twofold aspect.

>   "With an anvil-ding
> And with fire in him forge thy will
> Or rather, rather then, stealing as Spring
> Through him, melt him but master him still:
> Whether at once, as once at a crash Paul,
> Or as Austin, a lingering-out sweet skill,
>   Make mercy in all of us, out of us all
> Mastery, but be adored, but be adored King."

These verses bring to a conclusion the prologue which throughout has dealt with the various ways of recognising God's hand, of realising his presence in the Universe. Hopkins seems to suggest that since the Incarnation, since the time when Christ took on himself the form of man and lived a human life here in the world the earth has always kept traces of him: Nature has been sanctified. But this is a fact of which it is impossible to be aware constantly.

In the description of the storm which occupies four or five stanzas of the poem Hopkins excels: his verse communicates not only the appearance of the sinking ship and her passengers, their distress and dismay, but the very noise of the wind and waves, the hurry and scurry of the storm.

> "One stirred from the rigging to save
>   The wild woman-kind below,
> With a rope's end round the man, handy and brave—
>   He was pitched to his death at a blow,
> For all his dreadnought breast and braids of thew:
> They could tell him for hours, dandled the to and fro
> Through the cobbled foam-fleece, what could he do
> With the burl of the fountains of air, buck and the
>   flood of the wave?"

Then, before he describes the incident which particularly touched him, the nun calling upon Christ to come quickly, there is a lull in the poem, a moment of spiritual joy:

> "Ah! touched in your bower of bone
>   Are you! turned for an exquisite smart,
> Have you! make words break from me here all alone
>   Do you!—mother of being in me, heart.
> O unteachably after evil, but uttering truth,
> Why, tears! is it? tears; such a melting, a madrigal
>   start!
>   Never-eldering revel and river of youth,
> What can it be, this glee? the good you have there of
>   your own?"

It is not entirely spiritual joy; it is partly natural. Hopkins likes to observe the traces of good in human nature, remnants of the days before man had sinned. Here, in the spontaneous response which his heart makes to the action of the nun, he sees traces of the days when man was *naturally* good: as he does also in the later poem called *Brothers* where, describing the intense sympathy which the blood-bond creates in two boys, he takes pleasure in the beauty of natural affection:

> "Ah Nature, framed in fault,
> There's comfort then, there's salt:
> Nature, bad, base, and blind,
> Dearly thou canst be kind:
> There dearly thén, déarly,
> I'll cry thou canst be kind."

To return to the stanza in question: Hopkins excels in the description or rather the communication of moments of intense emotion. Of the artificiality which seems to me to be present in other parts of the poem there is no suspicion here. But when Hopkins turns, as he does presently, to discovering mysterious symbolisms and correspondences which link up this small instance of God's dealings with men, namely his treatment of the nuns, with his dealings as a whole—when he turns to discovering the general principle which lies behind this particular instance, the emotion which accompanies the intellect on its quest for symmetry does, I think, become forced, as in the verse:

> "She was first of a five and came
> Of a coifèd sisterhood.
> (O Deutschland, double a desperate name!
> O world wide of its good!

But Gertrude, lily, and Luther, are two of a town,
  Christ's lily and beast of the waste wood:
  From life's dawn it is drawn down,
Abel is Cain's brother and breasts they have sucked
    the same.)"

The assertion that good and bad often come from
the same source (provoked by the fact that the
heroic nun was a product of Protestant Germany)
might have been made in a much less emotional
tone: we feel that the poet is making too much fuss
about it. The fervour of the three following verses
also strikes the ear as a trifle exaggerated—that is to
say the reader suspects that fervour in the poem is
in excess of the fervour of the poet. But perhaps a
twentieth-century reader is too apt to be suspicious
of a poet who thinks it worth while to suggest
possible symbolic significance in the fact that the
number of the nuns was five.

  "Five! the finding and sake
And cipher of suffering Christ.
Mark, the mark is of man's make
And the word of it Sacrificed.
But he scores it in scarlet himself on his own be-
    spoken,
Before-time-taken, dearest-prizèd and priced—
  Stigma, signal, cinquefoil token
For lettering of the lamb's fleece, ruddying of the
    rose-flake."

The reader here is a little disconcerted by the sense
that the poet is writing with a seriousness which
suggests that he considers that the symbolism is one
which has an importance even outside the limits of

the poem: it has a significance for him which it lacks for the reader. But the verses in which he describes the mind's effort to discover the exact motive of the nun's cry illustrate Hopkins's excellence as clearly as they illustrate his originality. The last four stanzas of the poem are in Hopkins's grand style, a style which seems to exploit the resources of our language to the utmost.

Hopkins's "didactic" religious poetry is not his best, but as didactic poetry it is very good. The reader is apt to be rather on his guard when confronted by a poem which is evidently meant to teach him something and ready to take note of and be offended by any sign that the poet is speaking *de haut en bas*: the tone in didactic poetry is all important, and it is this which as a rule Hopkins manages so skilfully. *The Handsome Heart*, much as it has been praised and put into anthologies, is, I think, one of the few exceptions: it is also, I think, one of the few poems of his which can justly be charged with affectation. The self-consciousness of this poem is, I think, of the kind which is bad. Hopkins in his effort to trace in the boy the lineaments of sanctified human nature—the boy, like the Windhover and the storm fowl, is a creature who exhales or flashes out beauty merely by being what he is—falls into an awkwardness which recalls the infelicities of Wordsworth's style in his description of little Edward's behaviour in the *Anecdote for Fathers*. It seems, though, that while Wordsworth's awkwardness is due to a lack of self-criticism and self-consciousness, Hopkins's stiffness in this poem arises out of an excess of these qualities. If it is allowable to turn to French, the right word to describe *The Handsome Heart* is something like *guindé*. There is affectation in the very title of this sonnet: "The Handsome Heart: at a Gracious Answer". The poet is, I think, far less deeply touched by the incident than he takes himself to be: the charm and goodness of the boy's behaviour gratifies him as a priest and pleases him, too, because it illustrates a favourite theory of his. The frigidity which underlies the poem is revealed quite clearly in the utter flatness of the third line of the sestet:

"All, in this case, bathed in high hallowing grace",

and the forced playfulness with which he transfers the notion of buying the boy a present to the spiritual plane

"Of heaven what boon to buy you, boy?"

It is only, I think, when he comes to the last two lines of the sonnet, in which he is seized with fear for the boy's future, that the poem becomes alive:

"O on that path you pace
Run all your race, O brace sterner that strain."

He sees the boy as walking on the right path, but walking, not running, not realising how likely it is that he will be overtaken by some fearsome enemy unless he takes to his heels and does all he can, exerts himself to the utmost to get to the goal-post, to safety. At the moment he is only pacing, trying out his paces, making ready for the contest: the struggle and the danger are still to come. Hopkins seems always to have been roused to good poetry when he became conscious of his fears for the spiritual safety of the young. It is curious, by the way, to find Hopkins's very pronounced solicitude for what his biographer calls the "angelic virtue" of purity in the young echoed in a poem of Bridges called *Pater Filio*.

> "Sense with keenest edge unused
> Yet unsteel'd by scathing fire:
> Lovely feet as yet unbruised
> On the ways of dark desire:
> Sweetest hope that lookest smiling
> O'er the wilderness defiling!
>
> Why such beauty, to be blighted
> By the swarm of foul destruction?
> Why such innocence delighted,
> When sin stalks to thy seduction?
> All the litanies e'er chaunted
> Shall not keep thy faith undaunted."

The first two verses of Bridges's poem seem to have been written in a transport of apprehension, a mood which is less frequent with him than with Hopkins. "Sin stalks" is a phrase which suggests that Bridges was remembering Hopkins's fears for the bugler-boy: and it was perhaps his memory of the Jesuit which made him think of litanies and chaunting. Bridges's fears for his son are less controlled, and less under the domination of reason than Hopkins's fears for his young penitents. A symptom of this is that with all his contempt for litanies and chaunting—he mentions them rather in the manner of someone who thinks of them as pretty but insignificant pieces of ecclesiastical paraphernalia—he is wildly anxious that his son shall keep his faith. It is true that he is probably not using faith to mean belief in religious dogma: but the very vagueness of the term is symptomatic of the vague irrational nature of his fears. It is interesting to contrast this poem of Bridges with Hopkins's *On the Portrait of Two Beautiful Young People*. Hopkins, for all his profound foreboding, is never a prey to panic: if his emotions are naturally more violent than those of Bridges, it must also be said that he is better equipped to deal with violent emotion—in this case the emotion of fear. Bridges's *Pater Filio* has everything to lose, I think, from a comparison with the *Portrait of Two Beautiful Young People*: it is less good even than *The Bugler's First Communion*, with which it has much in common.

Often Hopkins evades the chief difficulty of the didactic poet: as it is himself whom he wishes to improve, there is no danger of his giving offence to the reader. In *The Candle Indoors* he takes pleasure, like Portia, in the light which a candle at some window or other throws on his path as he is walking at night: and he goes on hoping—all the more fervently because he will never know whether things are as he would wish or not—that behind the candle there is a Jessy or Jack, a man or woman, who, glorifying God in his or her words and works, puts back the dark in the same way. At this point the poet turns on himself:

"Come you indoors, come home; your fading fire
Mend first and vital candle in close heart's vault:
You there are master, do your own desire;
What hinders? Are you beam-blind, yet to a fault
In a neighbour deft-handed? are you that liar
And, cast by conscience out, spendsavour salt?"—

lines unsurpassed in vigour, concentration, and homeliness. He talks to himself without ceremony and familiarly as to one with whose failings he is well acquainted. This candle—unlike the one in the window—is of vital importance and it cannot be seen. There are no windows in the close heart's vault: there is no glory to be got by shewing that light. But that light it is in his power to make as bright as he wishes: he need not yearn for perfection in the candle indoors as he yearns for perfection in the Jessy or Jack behind the candle at the window. At home he is his own master: he can bring his desires to pass. Is it the truth that he is blind to his own great imperfections but keenly aware of the smallest room for improvement in others? The sharpness of the question at the end of the sonnet is terrifying. The words of the parable gain a great deal from Hopkins's arrangement of them: he has kept the cadences of speech and more—made it impossible to read the lines except so that the emphasis falls rightly.

The homeliness of Hopkins's language in *The Candle Indoors* is thoroughly in place. Hopkins seems, like Herbert, to have found that imagery of a homely concrete kind was often that best adapted to poems treating of spiritual matters.

But in *The Soldier* the homeliness of speech seems to me overdone. Hopkins writes with a bluff vigour which is not native to him and which is not effective in counteracting the sentimentality of the poem. It begins with a statement which has the air of being rather more than the truth—

"Yes. Whý do we áll, seeing of a soldier, bless him?
    bless
  Our redcoats, our tars..."

and goes on in the same vein, elaborating a parallel between our willingness to believe that the soldier still has some of the noble attributes which belong to his profession and Christ's readiness to see in Christians the qualities which belong to Christianity.

To What Serves Mortal Beauty is a very delicately balanced piece of work in which, without any pedantry on the one hand or sentimentality on the other, the poet explains how in his opinion we should behave in face of that beauty of person which an illiberal asceticism might consider nothing more than a snare. What is the good of it, this beauty which inflames the blood, the features that one longs to immortalise, the form which in its tautness is more majestic even than the dances suggested by the tunes of Purcell, the musician whom Hopkins

considered to have expressed the very make and
mind of man at its best?

"See: it does this: keeps warm
Men's wits to the things that are; | what good means
   —where a glance
Master more may than gaze,| gaze out of
   countenance."

It reminds men of the loveliness of God's creation,
keeps them from living in a selfish dream: it shews
them what the word *good* means: we acknowledge
beauty in a person instinctively and spontaneously:
we do not need to stare the beauty in the face and in
fact, as we are reminded by the phrase to look a
person out of countenance, under too close a
scrutiny the beauty may diminish: by our very
nature we respond immediately to personal beauty,
and it is, in Hopkins's opinion, a good thing that we
should do so, because it makes it likelier that our
nature will instinctively do homage to goodness. It
is natural and right to like the beautiful and to
single it out for admiration. If Gregory had not
responded to the attraction of the beauty of the
boy slaves England would not have been evangelised.
Christianity, says Hopkins, lays it down as in-
cumbent upon us to love men, God's living creation:
we must love them personally, love those marks of
unique individuality which every creature displays.
But not every unique individuality is beautiful:
what kind of preference, if any, are we to accord to
those that are? We are simply to pay them the
homage due: we must acknowledge that their beauty

is beauty; something which is one of God's good gifts must not be disregarded.

The mere prose substance of Hopkins's poetry has more value than that of much avowedly didactic or philosophical poetry. If by some disastrous decree all their respective poetical works were to be transmuted into prose paraphrases he would have the better, I think, of Browning and possibly of Wordsworth. *To What Serves Mortal Beauty* is a very polished poem, besides being a very original one. For all their odd appearance Hopkins's lines have an air of conversational ease: they might almost be called elegant.

Morning, Mid-day and Evening Sacrifice is not one of Hopkins's best poems. The first four lines give a charming picture of a young face:

> "The dappled die-away
> Cheek and wimpled lip,
> The gold-wisp, the airy-grey
> Eye—".

But the "all in fellowship" which follows suggests to me the ludicrous possibility that these features might have been at enmity. In my opinion a serious defect in the poem is the same "naked encounter of sensuality and asceticism" which Dr Bridges deprecates in *The Leaden Echo and the Golden Echo*. In these two poems Hopkins seems to conceive of the sacrifice of youth to Christ as involving actual immolation, spoliation of physical beauty. The poet lingers over the doomed beauty with something of

the slightly suspect and certainly Pagan pleasure
which leads Loret, the gazetteer of seventeenth-
century Paris, to describe in detail the charms of
those ladies of the court who are about to take the
veil:

> "Malgré tous ces riches appas
> Gallants, vous ne les aurez pas!"

This defect—if it is a defect except in the eyes of a
queasy twentieth century—is another trait which
Hopkins and Crashaw have in common: though in
Crashaw's poems "the naked encounter of sensuality and asceticism" is more often present than
not, and in Hopkins it only occurs four or five times.

The Leaden Echo and the Golden Echo is the
"Maiden's Song" from *St Winefred's Well*, the unfinished play of which other specimens are given in
Dr Bridges's edition of Hopkins's poems. Hopkins
thought highly of the poem, of which he wrote: "I
never did anything more musical". Mr T. Sturge
Moore, a poet austerer than Hopkins in his poetical
methods, offered the public a version of this poem in
which what appeared to him to be redundant was
pared off. But he himself, I think, confessed that,
though his own version seemed to him better, he had a
weakness for the original. If we are to take pleasure
in this poem we must take it as it stands: and it is as
baroque, as extravagant a piece of workmanship as
ever issued from the seventeenth century. The first
verse falls heavily, both in sound and in meaning,
representing as it does the Echo of Lead: the second
trips along with a rather precious grace, swaying

under its load of fluttering femininities. To say that the maidens are perhaps a little too self-consciously appreciative of the value of their young charms is to repeat Dr Bridges's criticism in a different form. It is more to the point here to praise the way in which Hopkins has exploited the musical resources of the language, contriving, with great ingenuity, never to sacrifice sense to sound. At the same time, great as the degree of technical accomplishment may be, *The Leaden Echo and the Golden Echo* is not one of the poems by which Hopkins may be said to stand or fall. It is more of a pretty piece than any other of his poems: in spite of all its charm it is somehow trivial. The imagery is often merely fanciful and there are single images which stand out from the texture of the poem as a whole, images of which the only justification is their ingenuity and which, worst of all, need to be justified before they can be enjoyed. It is possible, with some labour, to justify "fleece of beauty":

"flower of beauty, fleece of beauty, too too apt to,
    ah! to fleet."

The Golden Fleece which Jason found at Colchis was the prize given to beauty. So here "fleece" might be held to suggest supremacy in beauty. Again, the fleece which makes the sheep handsome is a thing of which in time it is very likely to be deprived: so that "fleece" might be said to repeat the notion of the transience of beauty which runs through the whole poem. In its context "fleece of beauty" might also be said to remind the reader appropriately that on leaving the world for the cloister the girl gives up her hair. But when all has been said the phrase remains a frigid one: the reader's instinctive motion is to reject it and when that is so, no justification of the kind given above can be very helpful: apart from the fact that it would be at least as easy to find reasons of that kind for rejecting the phrase—the function of the fleece is to keep the sheep warm, not to adorn it and so the word introduces the notion of utility which is out of keeping with beauty as it is conceived in the rest of the poem.

The didactic intention in *The Leaden and the Golden Echo* is very slight. The idea that whosoever loveth his youth shall lose it and whosoever resigns it willingly shall find it—

" Will have waked and have waxed and have walked
        with the wind what while we slept,
    This side, that side hurling a heavyheaded hun-
        dredfold
    What while we, while we slumbered. "—

is a tenuous theme almost overburdened with the variations which the poet plays on it. For the moment the particular tenet of Christianity of which he is treating is no more—if no less—vitally connected with himself than the idea contained, say, in the particular Celtic tale of which he is writing is with Mr Yeats.

But there are others of the poems which I have put in this class which are very much products of a religious poet. Hopkins derives intense pleasure from the moments when it seems to him clear that the God who works in Nature and the God who shews himself in Revelation are one: and the poems in which he works out a parallel between the air and the Blessed Virgin Mary, between the skylark in his cage and the soul in the body are not merely heartless exercises in metaphysical ingenuity. Take for instance the first of these poems, *The Blessed Virgin Compared to the Air we Breathe.* Here Hopkins considers the fact that as God provides us with air to maintain our bodily life, he made Mary the instrument. By which he gave us his Son who maintains in us spiritual life. The functions which they perform are very similar.

> "If I have understood,
> She holds high motherhood
> Towards all our ghostly good
> And plays in grace her part
> About man's beating heart,
> Laying, like air's fine flood,
> The deathdance in his blood."

Mary cools and calms our over-heated, too impetuous animal spirits so that the soul may have peace: as the freshness of the air cools our blood.

> "Again, look overhead
> How air is azurèd;
> O how! nay, do but stand
> Where you can lift your hand
> Skywards: rich, rich it laps
> Round the four finger gaps.
> Yet such a sapphire-shot
> Charged, steepèd sky will not

Stain light. Yea, mark you this:
It does no prejudice.
The glass-blue days are those
When every colour glows,
Each shape and shadow shows.
Whereas, did air not make
This bath of blue and slake
His fire, the sun would shake,
A blear and blinding ball
With blackness bound, and all
The thick stars round him roll
Flashing like flecks of coal,
Quartz-fret, or sparks of salt,
In grimy vasty vault."

We see God, in the second Person of the Trinity,
through Mary as we see the sun through the air.
Though the medium through which we see the sun
has a colour of its own, as Mary has a personality of
her own, this fact does not make it more difficult to
see through. On the contrary, it is only the presence
of the intermediary which prevents us from being
blinded.

The poet's mind is working in a similar way in
the *May Magnificat* which is a rationalisation of the
fact that God, acting through his Church, has chosen
to call the month of May the month of Mary. The
poet finds that the coming to life of Christ in Mary's
womb is aptly figured in the coming to life of earth
in spring, when:

"Cluster of bugle blue eggs thin
Forms and warms the life within;
And bird and blossom swell
In sod or sheathe or shell.

All things rising, all things sizing
Mary sees, sympathizing
   With that world of good,
   Nature's motherhood....

Their magnifying of each its kind
With delight calls to mind
   How she did in her stored
   Magnify the Lord."

(*Magnify*—literally, "go to swell", "go to make larger". Hopkins's pleasure in a pun—for I do not know what else to call it—of this kind is very characteristic.)

The substance of both these poems might be said to be nothing more than a conceit: but they are "conceits" which Hopkins has, in Keats's phrase, "proved upon his pulses". He does not work out the analogy in a mood of intellectual detachment: there is a calm of spirit underlying all his apparently freakish ingenuity and this is because for the moment by this apparently trivial piece of reasoning he has reached a certainty that in all the universe there are to be seen the workings of one spirit. The same confidence—a certainty which is really of the heart—is to be seen in the quietly majestic sonnet on St Alphonsus Rodriguez, the door-keeper saint whose sanctity brought him no renown. God was working in him as quietly as he works in the growth of flowers and of trees.

"Yet God (that hews mountain and continent,
  Earth, all, out; who, with trickling increment,

Veins violets and tall trees makes more and
    more)
Could crowd career with conquest while there
    went
Those years and years by of world without
    event
That in Majorca Alfonso watched the door."

The accumulation of tedium expressed in the phrase
"world without event" is most striking. We expect
the phrase to be "world without end" and so we
have the two phrases in our mind at the same time,
combining the notions of endlessness, monotonous-
ness, and resignation.

The same sober gladness expresses itself in the
sonnet beginning:

"As kingfishers catch fire, dragonflies draw flame."

I do not mean to suggest that it is the force of the
analogy between the way in which kingfishers catch
fire and the way in which the just man justices which
brings Hopkins peace of mind. The analogy is rather
the expression of a peace of mind already well
established. When the poet steps into what Wordsworth calls "a sort of oneness" it is natural to him
to yoke by violence together these dissimilar objects:
kingfishers, dragonflies, stones, bells and just men
all appear to him as fields in which works the one
Divine Providence: reality, to use his own phrase, is
for the moment unravelled, everything has become
gloriously clear. There is a sense of liberation behind
nearly all these poems in which by what appears

superficially to be nothing more than a conceit, God's workings in different aspects of the creation are seen to be similar.

But it is not always by working out an intellectual parallel between the two that Hopkins shews his longing to reconcile the world of Nature and the world of the spirit as the Christian conceives it. The poems which I have put in the first class all deal in an intellectual way with something which is more or less in the nature of a maxim or aphorism: and however much the maxim has been proved upon Hopkins's pulses the poem cannot be said to deal directly with religious experience. Turning to those poems which are records of experience, which deal with moods rather than with maxims, we find Hopkins rushing with a great bound of the heart from the natural to the spiritual, as if in the hope of abolishing all barriers between the two. Take, for instance, the lovely childlike poem which he calls *The Starlight Night.* The ecstasy which takes possession of him as he looks up at the starlit sky is not at first one in which the soul is concerned. His mind and body thrill at the sight of the starry skies, as Wordsworth's did when he looked over the vale of Grasmere in the early morning. Even when he has diverted the ecstasy into a religious channel he does not deny Nature her due. The sight which he has before him is so beautiful that he will not say that it is merely the type of the reward: it *is* the reward. However, by making the starry sky the outermost wall of heaven he rationalises his rapture. The skies are only lovely because Christ is lovely. Hopkins is never so happy as when he feels that the beauty of God and Nature are the same.

Most of Hopkins's best poems are found in the second class, namely of those which deal directly with his relationship with Christ. Of these *The Windhover*, the poem which Hopkins considered his best and dedicated to our Lord, deserves first consideration.

THE WINDHOVER

To Christ our Lord

I caught this morning morning's minion, king-
dom of daylight's dauphin, dapple-dawn-drawn
  Falcon, in his riding
Of the rolling level underneath him steady air, and
  striding
High there, how he rung upon the rein of a wimpling
  wing
In his ecstasy! then off, off forth on swing,
As a skate's heel sweeps smooth on a bow-bend: the
  hurl and gliding
Rebuffed the big wind. My heart in hiding
Stirred for a bird,—the achieve of, the mastery of
  the thing!

Brute beauty and valour and act, oh, air, pride,
  plume, here
Buckle! AND the fire that breaks from thee then,
  a billion
Times told lovelier, more dangerous, O my chevalier!

No wonder of it: shéer plód makes plough down
   sillion
Shine, and blue-bleak embers, ah my dear,
Fall, gall themselves, and gash gold-vermilion.

The Windhover, like most very great poetry, has
had many different meanings attributed to it. This
partly because it is so rich in significance and partly
because the poet's state of mind is one in which two
contradictory moods are held in equipoise and the
reader can make one or the other predominate as
he chooses: as a piece of shot silk will appear to be
silver when held in one light and black when held
in another. I give my own interpretation, one to
which I have become so accustomed that it seemed
to me that anybody reading the poem must see
that as far as the poem had a plain straightforward
meaning it was this:

The poet is overwhelmed by the beauty of the
kestrel. The bird is the darling of the element in
which it moves, the day which serves as a background to its exploits. Everything gives way to the
creature, intent as it is on performing its own
peculiar function. Brute beauty, courage, act, air,
the bird's pride in itself, the power of flying, are all
contracted, buckled within the small span of the
bird's body: all these things buckle to, set to, that
the bird may fly and wheel as its nature directs it:
all buckle, give way, collapse, beneath the bird's
dominant impulse.

If the stress is laid on *thee*, the next lines must be
taken as coming from Christ. When you subject,

says Christ, addressing the poet, all your faculties and all material obstacles to your desire to do the thing which you were meant to do, the fire, the beauty which to my eyes follows in your wake is a thousand times greater than that of the trail left by the kestrel. (The notion that all creatures are at their loveliest when they are exerting all their faculties to the utmost recurs in Hopkins's poetry. He speaks of a sailor's limbs as being "strung by duty, strained to beauty", and in the sonnet to Purcell the colours which strike from the bird's plumage as he flies illustrate the fact that beauty is a by-product, flashed off accidentally by a creature intent only on performing its own peculiar function.)

Taking the stress in the ninth line as falling on *then*, Christ must be taken as apostrophising the kestrel. When you compel all your faculties to exert themselves to the utmost, when you disregard everything except the performance of the exploits for which you were born: at that moment your powers are at their highest and your loveliness is a thousand times greater and more formidable than it was before you put aside all thought of it in order to do your work.

The poet, hearing these words of Christ's, says meekly and resignedly, but sorrowfully, that that is always so. The maxim applies not only to creatures of splendid fire and power, such as the kestrel, but to things which move slowly and with pain. The heavy plough, as it makes its way through the earth, sends off the gleam of steel: and the ashes of the wood-

fire, which are not meant to do anything beyond
suffering themselves to fall to the ground, as they do
this break open and disclose colours of red and gold.
It is evidently the wood-fire which represents the
condition of the poet himself. The poet assents to
the words of comfort: there is no doubt, he seems to
say, that it is true that to Christ the spectacle of the
kestrel is no lovelier than the sight of the dying fire,
though the function of the former is performed with
joy to the creature itself and that of the latter with
pain: but there is a suggestion in the undertones of
the poem that the words of comfort have not quite
gone home: the poet is still envious of the beauty of
the bird. In the "Ah my dear" (a phrase which he
took from Herbert—

"I the unkind, the ungrateful? Ah my dear
    I cannot look on Thee")

with which he submits himself, sighing, to Christ
there is a suggestion of reproach which is no less
reproachful because it is tender. How can Christ
choose to leave his creature in such anguish, the poet
seems to ask. It is clear then that there may be
many and very different interpretations of this one
poem.

But on comparing my reading with Dr Richards's
much fuller and more fluid interpretation of the
poem it becomes evident that the former, in spite of
all my efforts to the contrary, remains purely personal. Here is Dr Richards's version:

"'Caught' is here partly, no doubt, to introduce
this astonishing series: 'dauphin, dapple-dawn-

drawn Falcon' which, taking up 'this morning
morning's minion, kingdom' begins the simulation
of the falcon's sustained, even and returning, flight.
The rhymes evidently repeat its curves. But the
'I' as first word makes it from the outset—the first
glimpse of the marvel—a spiritual adventure, *not*
a description with a moral, or a parable excogitated
out of a recollection. The poet is participating in the
miracle of the bird's flight: empathy could hardly
be taken further in verse; and when, in the seventh
line, he turns to consider himself, it is because something extraordinary has already happened. 'My
heart in hiding stirred for a bird.'

"A turning point, with me, for the interpretation
of the poem, is in the phrase 'in hiding'. 'In
hiding' from what and how and why? These are
questions so wide that a score of different persons'
different meditations upon them at different stages
in their lives would hardly do more than indicate
their scope. The shock of the internal rhyme
'stirred for a bird' conveys, for me, the poet's own
astonishment that he has been so moved, so
awakened, so shaken by something which, in comparison with the supreme subject of his usual daily
devotions and exercises, seems so slight a thing;
and the rest of the line is the first commonplace
insufficient rationalisation of the experience, the
ordinary self-protection explanation of the cause of
this emotion.

"But the phrase 'in hiding' has already shown
that—without some deep personal application, some
parallel in the inner essential preoccupations and
purposes of his own life—the mere perception of the
perfection of the bird's flight, its supremacy of self-
controlled audacity, is not enough. After a pause,

(134)

he gives the development. For me, most often, though not with any finality or fixity, this development seems to hang upon the words 'in hiding'. The feeling of the last six lines changes shimmeringly through a wide range of colours as the lingering sense of 'in hiding' shifts with the different possibilities that 'then' and the comparatives 'lovelier, more dangerous' bring out. A prose indication of these fixes them in greater independence and sharper opposition than they possess in the rapid co-presentation of the poem.

"The poet's heart has been in hiding, from the life of the senses, from the life of imagination and emotional risk, from speculation...It has been hiding in the routine of meditation, in doctrine taken as understood or left unexplored, in the seeming security of a won shelter. Not riding abroad 'O my chevalier'; not trusting itself to its gift to be held up at dangerous heights by the gale it knows how to master if it will, it has sunk into a lethargy, shrinking from the toil of preparation for a rebirth. As plough to itself, it has grown rusty; as fuel to its own spirit, it has forgotten to burn. In the shock of an admiration, an envy, of this symbol of free, perilous, triumphant flight, and with a pang of regret for the renunciations of physical adventure imposed by his choice of life—something slips, as a coal on a dying fire. Wounded, he is again alight, or he would be, with the kingly tragic passion of his renewed vocation. A passion, 'lovelier, more dangerous', as shared by his chevalier, whom he now more understands and to whom, I take it, 'ah my dear' is addressed—than is given in any natural adventure or any windless travel. But the shock of self-realisation has still been a wound, a breaking of something, Mr Empson's secondary sense for 'buckle' may have its place. Certainly the movement of the last three lines is weary, something like despair has not been far off. There has been a new renunciation, an effort of the will, which leaves him, the last line shows it, exhausted. Though conceived and conveyed in such personal terms, the experience seems to have an unrestricted universality. The symbolism of 'kingdom of daylight's dauphin'—Son of the Sun, flashing with reflected fire—does not diminish it. At the end the contrast between that fire and the labour and self-consumption ('world's wild-fire, leave but ash') of the following hours, extends its reference indefinitely:

'We hear our hearts grate on themselves: it kills
To bruise them dearer.'"

Mr Empson, in his *Seven Types of Ambiguity*[1] adds more points to the analysis of the poem.

"Hopkins became a Jesuit and burnt his early poems on entering the order: there may be some reference to this sacrifice in the *fire* of the Sonnet. Confronted suddenly with the active physical beauty of the bird, he conceives it as the opposite of his patient spiritual renunciation: the statements of the poem appear to insist that his own life is superior but he cannot decisively judge between them and holds both with agony in his mind. 'My heart in hiding' would seem to imply that the more dangerous life is that of the Windhover, but the last three lines insist it is no wonder that the life of renunciation should be the more lovely. 'Buckle' admits of two tenses and two meanings: 'they do buckle here' or 'come, buckle yourself here'; buckle,

[1] Published by Chatto and Windus.

like a military belt, for the discipline of heroic action, and buckle like a bicycle wheel, 'make useless, distorted and incapable of its natural motion'. 'Here' may mean in the case of the bird or in the case of the Jesuit; then 'when you have become like the bird' or 'when you have become like the Jesuit.' Chevalier personifies either physical or spiritual activity: Christ riding to Jerusalem, or the cavalryman ready for the charge; Pegasus, or the Windhover.

"Thus in the first three lines of the sestet we seem to have a clear case of the Freudian use of opposites, where two things thought of as incompatible but desired intensely by different systems of judgments are spoken of simultaneously by words applying to both: both desires are thus given a transient and exhausting satisfaction, and the two systems of judgment are forced into open conflict before the reader. Such a process, one might imagine, could pierce to regions that underlie the whole structure of our thought: could tap the energies of the very depths of the mind. At the same time one may doubt whether it is most effective to do it so crudely as in these three lines: this enormous conjunction standing as it were for the point of friction between the two worlds conceived together affects one rather like shouting in an actor and probably to many readers the lines seem so meaningless as to have no effect at all. The last three lines which profess to come to a single judgment on the matter, convey the conflict more strongly and more beautifully.

"The metaphor of the fire covered by ash seems most to insist on the beauty the fire gains when the ash falls in, when its precarious order is again shattered: perhaps too, on the pleasure, in that some movement, some risk, even to so determinedly static a prisoner, is still possible. The gold that painters have used for the haloes of saints is forced by alliteration to agree with the gash and gall of their self-tortures: from this precarious triumph we fall again, with vermilion to bleeding."

Mr Empson perhaps sacrifices something of the value of the poem to his desire to make it illustrate the Freudian doctrine of which he has been reminded: the crudity which he ascribes to the first three lines of the sestet would not exist in the poem as interpreted by Dr Richards. I think too that his interpretation suggests that Hopkins was unnaturally conscious of the strangeness of his being a Jesuit; that he saw himself as a rather stagey if pathetic figure: I should be sorry to give exclusively liturgical associations to gold, gash and gall: here again Mr Empson seems to me to suggest that Hopkins was rather self-consciously Catholic, or in Hügel's phrase, churchy. To me it seems that Hopkins's poems are the product of a sensibility which was far too mature and healthy to allow him to take a disproportionate pleasure in ecclesiastical paraphernalia. An exception may be made of *Elected Silence*, a poem which is very much the work of the kind of person conjured up by the phrase "undergraduate convert". The associations suggested by Mr Empson to me limit unnecessarily the implications of the sonnet. Hopkins's best poetry is the product of a very catholic Catholicism and when his experience is at its most intense, as in *The Windhover*, it is also most universal.

Mr Herbert Read in the article in *New Verse* to which I have already alluded has some rather mystifying remarks on *The Windhover*. "*The Windhover* is completely objective in its senseful catalogue; but Hopkins gets over his scruples by dedicating the poem To Christ our Lord. But this is a patent deception. It does not alter the naked sensuality of the poem. There is no asceticism in this poem: nor, essentially, in any of the other poems in this group. They are tributes to God's glory, as all poetry must be: but they are tribute of the senses; and a right conception of God and of religion will not be hurt by such." It is for Mr Read to prove that Hopkins had scruples about the poem, that Hopkins's conception of religion was the mistaken one which thinks that asceticism alone is pleasing to God. He scarcely does this, I think, by quoting Hopkins's remark about Keats. It is surely possible to hold that "the poet...by nature a dreamer and a sensualist only raises himself to greatness by concerning himself with great causes as liberty and religion" without believing that only ascetic poetry is justified. Hopkins's actual criticisms of Keats is this:

"It is impossible not to feel with weariness how his verse is at every turn abandoning itself to an unmanly and enervating luxury. It appears too that he said something like 'O for a life of impressions instead of thoughts!' It was, I suppose, the life he tried to lead. The impressions are not likely to have been all innocent, and they soon ceased in death. His contemporaries, as Wordsworth, Byron, Shelley, and even Leigh Hunt, right or wrong, still concerned themselves with great causes, as liberty and religion; but he lived in mythology and fairyland, the life of a dreamer: nevertheless, I feel and see in him the beginnings of something opposite to this, of an interest in higher things, and of powerful and active thought. Nor do I mean that he would have turned to a life of virtue—only God can know that—but that his genius would have taken to an austerer utterance in art. Reason, thought, what he did not want to live by, would have asserted itself presently and perhaps have been as much more powerful than that of his contemporaries as his sensibility or impressionableness, by which he did want to live, was keener and richer than theirs. His defects were due to youth—the self-indulgence of his youth, its ill-education, and also, as it seems to me, to its breadth and pregnancy, which, by virtue of a fine judgment already able to restrain but unable to direct, kept him from flinging himself blindly on the specious liberal stuff that crazed Shelley, and indeed in their youth, Wordsworth and Coleridge."[1]

Surely Hopkins's criticism of Keats shews no particularly strong tendency to asceticism, certainly no inclination to hold that without asceticism in the poet there can be no great poetry. It is very generally thought and by people not in the least ascetic, I should say, that great poetry can only be written by men who "see life steadily and see it whole", who cut themselves off from none of the major activities of human beings: Hopkins's pronounce-

[1] *Life*, by G. F. Lahey, p. 74.

ment on Keats seems to me to be no more ascetic
than Keats's pronouncement on himself.

> "First the realm I'll pass
> Of Flora and old Pan: sleep in the grass.
> Feed upon apples red, and strawberries,
> And choose each pleasure that my fancy sees;...
>
> And can I ever bid these joys farewell?
> Yes, I must pass them for a nobler life,
> Where I may find the agonies, the strife
> Of human hearts...."   *Sleep and Poetry.*

I sometimes suspect that we are many of us so certain
that becoming a Jesuit must involve some unnatural
and undesirable deformation or repression that we
are prepared to see oddities in a Jesuit poet where
there are none. Mr Read, however, seems to suggest
that although Hopkins had actually suffered no ill
effects from following his vocation, he was compelled
nevertheless to disguise from himself the fact that his
sensibility continued to be healthy, his senses keen.
I must confess that I see no unmistakable sign that
Hopkins was morbidly ashamed of his natural man:
certainly there is none in *The Windhover*. If there is
a poem which contains such a suggestion it is the
sonnet beginning "The shepherd's brow fronting
forked lightning" which Dr Bridges in his edition
relegated to the section containing fragments and
unfinished poems, because he thought it the product
of a passing mood which Hopkins would not wish to
perpetuate. I think there is no doubt that towards
the end of his life Hopkins was haunted from time to

time, especially in moments of extreme mental fatigue, by an overwhelming sense of self-disgust. But Hopkins certainly did not encourage this mood as presumably he would have done if he had felt it the product of an asceticism particularly pleasing to God: he seems on the contrary to consider it highly irreligious. The sonnet to which I have referred is the only poem in which he indulges it fully. There is no disguising the fact that religion does play some part in this mood of self-disgust—

"Angels fall, they are towers, from heaven—a story
Of just, majestical and giant groans.
But man—we, scaffold of score brittle bones;
Who breathe, from groundlong babyhood to hoary
Age gasp; whose breath is our *memento mori*—
What bass is *our* viol for tragic tones?
He! Hand to mouth he lives, and voids with shame...."

Hopkins is overwhelmed by something of the disgust with the human species which attacked Swift: the sonnet shews a morbid detestation of human limitations and of these evidently his religion makes him more than usually aware. But it may also be said that when he was in such a mood as that if there had been no angels he would have been driven to invent them: or at least some other species of perfect, august, and infallible beings whose perfection should serve to make clearer the repulsive triviality of his own kind. I cannot think that Hopkins's despondency was a particularly religious one: the analogy is with Swift, not with Cowper. His self-disgust is not, as far as one can judge, the distorted product of an exaggerated humility: his religion, though it may supply material on which to exercise his disgust, is in no way the cause of it.

The sonnet is not a successful poem, I think, though it has great interest as a psychological record. His feelings for once get the better of him; he has not been able to achieve the control which makes Cowper's *The Castaway*, for instance, an excellent poem in spite of the state of mind which produced it. In those of his good poems into which the self-disgust enters it is always kept under control: when he is most devout he is most on his guard against it—take for instance the beautiful

"My own heart let me have more pity on; let
   Me live to my sad self hereafter kind,
   Charitable; not live this tormented mind
   With this tormented mind tormenting yet...",

a sonnet in which he talks to himself in homely comforting tones, treats himself with something of the charity which he might use towards a penitent. It is very difficult to agree with Mr Read's suggestion that Hopkins had a deep-rooted conviction that an exaggerated asceticism is what is most pleasing to God. Hopkins's conception of religion seems to me admirable as much for its reasonableness as for its devotion.

As I have already said, Hopkins's devotional attitude has much more in common with that of

Eliot than with that of Herbert. Herbert's attitude towards God is marked by a childlike confidence, springing perhaps from a sense that he is so much loved that estrangement is impossible: and this trustfulness prevents him from ever sinking quite as low in despondency as Hopkins does. A loving familiarity, which never loses its balance and topples into irreverence, characterises both these poets in their intercourse with the Divine: but there is very little that is coaxing or childlike in Hopkins's devotional poems, as there is constantly in Herbert's. Herbert at times becomes almost cajoling in his efforts to persuade God to relax his severity.

> "Throw away Thy rod.
> Though man frailties hath
>   Thou art God;
> Throw away Thy wrath."

The only one of Hopkins's poems which is marked throughout by a tender ingenuousness such as we expect from Herbert is his translation of St Francis Xavier's hymn—*O Deus ego amo te.*

> "Then I, why should not I love thee,
> Jesu, so much in love with me?
> Not for heaven's sake; not to be
> Out of hell by loving thee;
> Not for any gains I see;
> But just the way that thou didst me
> I do love and I will love thee;
> What must I love thee, Lord, for then?
> For being my King and God. Amen."

But on the whole Herbert is much more of "a little

(144)

child" in his devotional poems than the nineteenth-century poet found it possible to be. The elements of their spiritual experience are roughly the same. Herbert does not find the life he has chosen any easier than Hopkins found his. His quaintness should not mislead us into forgetting that he too had the sense of being thwarted and deserted: Hopkins's *Justus quidem te* may very well be compared with Herbert's poem called *The Cross*:

"What is this strange and uncouth thing...."

Again, Hopkins's sonnet, "I wake and feel the fell of dark, not day", the most majestic, the bleakest of all his sonnets, may be compared with one of the many poems of Herbert's which are called *Affliction*, that in which his reproaches suddenly give way to a protestation of the staunchest affection. He enumerates his grievances one by one: in the last verse it becomes apparent that the only thing to do is to renounce this relationship altogether.

"Well, I will change the service and go seek
Some other Master out."

But the revulsion which this proposal excites in him makes it clear to him that, for all his sense of grievance, his heart is fixed and he protests impulsively:

"Ah, my dear God, though I be clean forgot,
Let me not love Thee, if I love Thee not."

It is by the heart that Herbert is held; Hopkins in his moments of desolation seems to keep hold of faith only by the reason and the will. His suffering is the suffering of a soul which is more adult than Herbert's. His poetry comes up from profounder depths than Herbert ever sounded. In this instance it is by the labour of his reason, not, as with Herbert, by a spontaneous impulse of affection, that Hopkins is brought back to acquiescence in his relationship with God.

> "I wake and feel the fell of dark, not day.
> What hours, O what black hoürs we have spent
> This night! What sights you, heart, saw; ways you
>   went!
> And more must, in yet longer light's delay."

The night seems interminable, like the night of the soul, which now becomes the poet's theme. His complaint goes on, accumulating causes of sadness, until at last, in the exaggeration forced on him by despair, he claims that he knows while still alive the torments of the damned.

> "I see
> The lost are like this, and their scourge to be
> As I am mine, their sweating selves."

But at this point, as in Herbert's poem, there comes a change of attitude—not however, like Herbert's, a complete *volte-face*, not an impetuous somersault. His attitude is modified by the intervention of self-criticism: his scrupulous judgment points out that, after all, what he has just been saying cannot be quite true. "But worse", he adds: and the tragic complaint comes to an end with the admission that he has been talking wildly and that there is, in spite of everything, still room for hope. That, of course, is only one of the possible interpretations of the poem: "but worse" is a cryptic phrase, and in the work of a poet who deliberately ignored customary syntax it may very well be taken to apply to his own condition, instead of to that of the lost: although I think that that interpretation would always be subordinated to the other. Hopelessness is in the undertone: the overtone conveys the return of hope. There is, as Mr Empson has pointed out, an ambiguity of something the same kind in Herbert's poem. But the ambiguity in Herbert's poem is much nearer the surface: one feels that he is in a position to think of the words as words and to enjoy playing with them. The ambiguity in Hopkins seems to be unconscious and involuntary: one remembers his saying that these sonnets came "unbidden and against his will". It must be seldom that experiences of such profundity and complexity become articulate. In these sonnets in spite of the surface strangeness of Hopkins's work the reader finds himself paying little attention to the words as words: there is no temptation to criticise the poet's expressions, scarcely any possibility of standing aloof from the experience in order to criticise. The experience behind these four involuntary sonnets and that behind *The Windhover* impose themselves on the reader with peculiar force. It becomes almost as difficult for the reader to resist the experience as it was for Hopkins. These poems have a contagiousness which one would expect to belong only to moods of ecstatic abandon. But in the moment of most intense emotion, Hopkins never loses his self-consciousness or rather, for there should be no pejorative implication, his self-awareness: he is acutely conscious of what is happening and in this consciousness a certain amount of self-criticism is implicit.

Matthew Arnold says that the situations, from the representation of which, though accurate, no poetical enjoyment can be derived, are those "in which the suffering finds no vent in action; in which a continuous state of mental distress is prolonged, unrelieved by incident, hope or resistance: in which there is everything to be endured, nothing to be done.... When they occur in actual life, they are painful also". The situation which produced Hopkins's best poetry seems to be very near to that which Arnold describes: and it is true, I think, that Hopkins's poetry never achieves the tragic: *The Windhover* itself does not leave the reader purged: he is rather pierced. A poignant pathos is Hopkins's characteristic quality. Hopkins's suffering seems to be of the kind which "finds no vent in action": but he finds some sort of outlet in the cultivation of an intense and precise awareness of all that is going on in him. Perhaps it is because of this habit that he is able to make use even of the kind of situation which Arnold describes as not lending itself to poetry: Hopkins seems to have known no kind of pain which could not be made to yield occasions for poetical enjoyment. Yet no one perhaps was ever unhappier in his unhappiness than Hopkins seems to have been: he had no way of escaping from sorrow: so far from cultivating insensibility, like Webster's Flamineo—

"We endure the strokes like anvil or hard steel
  Till pain itself make us no pain to feel"—

Hopkins seems to have progressed in exactly the opposite direction, developing more and more new capacities of pain:

"Pitched past pitch of grief,
More pangs will, schooled at forepangs, wilder wring."

But his cultivation of intense and precise consciousness of the kind of experience which he is undergoing, though it does not provide him with a means of escaping from his distress, does give him a sense of being, if not in control of the situation, at least not wholly passive: and it is this consciousness of the exact nature of his experience which makes his poetry.

Hopkins's work is never better than in the "terrible" sonnets and *The Windhover*. They represent the deepest point touched by his poetry, which runs in a channel exceptionally pure and deep; though it is not, like Shakespeare's, a springing river with many tributaries. Using Arnold's touchstone method, the critic might easily find that Hopkins's best poetry is not dimmed or made to seem trivial by comparison with the best of Shakespeare and Dante. He has not their variety but his best poetry is not inferior to theirs in kind. Arnold's phrase "high seriousness" describes most justly the quality of Hopkins's greatest poems. His poetry is that of a man with exceptional intelligence and exceptional sensibility, who is constantly taking into account all the facts of his experience; he uses religion not as a solution but as an approach, a way of keeping all the facts in mind without losing sanity.

It would be a great pity if Hopkins came to be generally thought of as a poet for the few, for those willing to take disproportionate trouble in order to enjoy the work of a brilliant eccentric, or for those drawn to him by a common religion, only. In spite of the peculiarities of his mind and circumstances, Hopkins in his best work comes as near as, say, Dante, to making his experience available to all: he merits the extreme of popularity which he himself, a critic as just as modest, thought his due.

For EU product safety concerns, contact us at Calle de José Abascal, 56–1°, 28003 Madrid, Spain or eugpsr@cambridge.org.

www.ingramcontent.com/pod-product-compliance
Ingram Content Group UK Ltd.
Pitfield, Milton Keynes, MK11 3LW, UK
UKHW012327130625
459647UK00009B/125